C000246229

THE BEST OF THE

SEX MAGICK

SEX MAGICK

VOLUME III

ALEISTER CROWLEY
Introduction by Lon Milo DuQuette

WEISER BOOKS
San Francisco, CA / Newburyport, MA

This edition first published in 2013 by Weiser Books
Red Wheel/Weiser, LLC
With offices at:
665 Third Street, Suite 400
San Francisco, CA 94107
www.redwheelweiser.com

ISBN: 978-1-57863-571-9

Library of Congress Cataloging-in-Publication Data is available upon
request.

Cover design by Jim Warner
Cover photograph © Ordo Templi Orientis. Used by permission.
Interior by Frame25 Productions
Printed in the United States of America

EBM
10 9 8 7 6 5 4 3 2 1

The paper used in this publication meets the minimum requirements
of the American National Standard for Information Sciences—
Permanence of Paper for Printed Library Materials Z39.48-1992
(R1997).

CONTENTS

INTRODUCTION

For I am divided for love's sake, for the chance
of union. This is the creation of the world, that
the pain of division is as nothing, and the joy of
dissolution all.

Liber AL vel Legis, I, 29 & 30.

Also, take your fill and will of love as ye will, when,
where and with whom ye will! But always unto me.

Liber AL vel Legis, I, 51.

When you have proved that God is merely a name
for the sex instinct, it appears to me not far to the
perception that the sex instinct is God.

Aleister Crowley – The Equinox III: 1.

I n June of 1912 a thirty-four-year-old Aleister Crowley
received a strange and colorful visitor to his London
flat at 124 Victoria Street. The mysterious caller was Herr
Theodor Reuss, agent of the Prussian Secret Service,
Wagnerian opera singer,[1] newspaper correspondent, high
degree Freemason, and head of *Ordo Templi Orientis,* a

---

1 In 1882 he sang at Bayreuth at the premier of Wagner's *Parsifal.*

German magical society with Rosicrucian and Masonic pretentions. Two years earlier Reuss had presented Crowley with honorary membership in the O.T.O., presumably in hopes it would bolster Crowley's esoteric credentials in a lawsuit that had been filed against him by S. L. MacGregor Mathers, the head of the London-based Hermetic Order of the Golden Dawn.

Mathers had sued to prevent Crowley from publishing proprietary initiation rituals and teachings of the G.D. in his publication, *The Equinox*. In the suit, Mathers was claiming to be the worldwide head of the "Rosicrucians," an act of spiritual presumption which outraged Reuss and the leaders of a score of other existing European Hermetic and Rosicrucian societies. In an attempt to dilute Mathers' credentials in the eyes of the court these organizations lavished a host of honorary degrees and titles upon Crowley—so many that he completely lost track of his various memberships, degrees and mystic titles. Crowley eventually won the suit and published *The Equinox*.

The purpose of the June, 1912 visit from Reuss, however, was not to discuss the lawsuit or Golden Dawn matters, but to take Crowley to task for publishing the O.T.O.'s supreme secret of sexual magick. Crowley protested that he had done no such thing, and that in fact, he didn't even know the secret and was completely unaware that the O.T.O. had anything to do with sex magick.

Reuss stepped to Crowley's own bookshelf and plucked out a copy of *Liber CCCXXXIII: The Book of Lies*[2] and opened it to chapter 36, *The Star Sapphire*, a short version of the Hexagram Ritual.

Crowley did not immediately understand exactly how the contents of this tiny chapter could possibly reveal the supreme secret of sexual magick, so Ruess patiently discussed what he had written *vis a vis* certain theoretical and aspects of magick. He led the discussion in such a way that Crowley experienced an almost instant epiphany. He was stunned. Since childhood he had intuited the importance and the potential power of sex. But here, in the most profound and simple terms, was the key – not only to the mythological symbolism of the ancients, of Christianity and Freemasonry, but (theoretically at least) the key to the mysteries of human consciousness and creation itself.

Before the afternoon had passed, Ruess had conferred upon Crowley (and his lover, Leila Waddell) the highest initiatory degree of the O.T.O., the IX°, and obligated them to the discretionary terms of its communication. This 'oath of secrecy' is a somewhat paradoxical obligation. Rather than being an oath *not* to reveal the secret to the world, it is rather more a promise to

---

2 Aleister Crowley. *Liber CCCXXXIII: The Book of Lies Which Is Also Falsely Called Breaks, the Wanderings or Falsifications of the One Thought of Frater Perdurabo, Which Thought Is Itself Untrue.* The original publication date was most likely purposefully mislabeled 1913. First published with commentary copyright © 1962 Ordo Templi Orientis. (York Beach, ME: Red Wheel/Weiser 1987).

perpetuate the secret, to assure that it is protected, preserved, and never profaned, diluted, corrupted or lost.

One doesn't learn a true magical secret like one learns a juicy piece of gossip. A true magical secret is a light bulb that goes off over your own head when you finally "get" something. In other words, the IX° initiate of the O.T.O. is not obligated to conceal the "secret" but on the contrary, obligated to make sure as many worthy individuals as possible discover the secret by discerning it themselves.

Crowley took this obligation very seriously, and his writings on this particular subject (as we will see in this *Best of the Equinox* volume on Sex Magick) can be very difficult to understand. They are full of strange, sometimes disturbing and confusing symbolic language that Crowley believed clearly *revealed everything* there was to reveal to *anyone ready* to have *everything revealed* to them.

I must confess, this is not easy. But it is a magical labor well worth the effort, because the reward is nothing less than the Holy Grail itself.

After bestowing the IX° on Crowley and Leila, Ruess also authorized Crowley to create and head a British chapter of O.T.O. and directed him to expand and develop the organization's rituals of initiation into workable and viable magical ceremonies. From that moment until the end of his life in 1947 sex magick would be the focus of Aleister Crowley's magical work.

Unfortunately, the term, *sex magick*, has a somewhat lurid ring to it. It brings to mind visions of costumed orgies and pornographic acts of dramatic depravity.

Crowley's outrageous and eccentric lifestyle and reputation did little to assuage public perceptions about the naughtiness of anything he might be involved in. It's true, he enjoyed shocking anyone who was easy to shock. To the disappointment of many would-be magicians, however, sex magick is a demanding physical and meditative yogic discipline of the highest order. The underlying theory of the technique is as challenging to the imagination as the postulates of quantum mechanics. Yet the fundamental key to sex magick is breathtakingly simple, and can be summarized in the single word "ecstasy" – the divine consciousness we all experience whenever we temporarily obliterate our sense of separateness from Godhead in timeless moments of orgasm. In that eternal instant the self becomes the *All* – and when we are the All . . . there is *nothing* we cannot create.

Modern students of Crowley are further challenged by the terminology he was obliged to use in order to camouflage a direct discussion of the subject. Such obfuscation was necessary not only because of Crowley's O.T.O. obligations, but also because of serious concerns of legality. We must recall that it wasn't so very long ago that one could not legally publish material concerning sexual matters. Even medical journals needed to be very careful about how the subject was approached in print. Ironically, discussions of human/blood sacrifice were not taboo subjects to write about. Crowley was fiendishly delighted to play this game of words with the publishing world and the public. Not to be dissuaded, he simply drew upon his mastery of language and his knowledge of the colorful metaphors of magick to be as shockingly explicit as he wanted. He (sometimes unwisely) assumed any moderately intelligent person would know what he was really saying.

Orgasm and ecstasy he could refer to as *death* and *sacrifice*; sexual fluids (sacred elements used as Eucharistic talismans in India and the East for millennia) became *blood* or *water* or the *elixir*; the penis became the *lance*, or the *wand*, or the *rood*, or the *cross*; the vagina the *cup*, or the *grail*, or the *rose*, etc.

In *Magick in Theory and Practice* Crowley confesses exactly what kind of game he is playing. In Chapter 12, *Of the Bloody Sacrifice, and of Matters Cognate,* he writes,

> You are also likely to get into trouble over this chapter unless you truly comprehend its meaning.*

He also begins a footnote to the above statement by warning the reader,

> *There is a traditional saying that whenever an Adept seems to have made a straightforward, comprehensible statement, then is it most certain that He means something entirely different. The Truth is nevertheless clearly set forth in His Words; it is His simplicity that baffles the unworthy. I have chosen the expressions in this Chapter in such a way that it is likely to mislead those

Magicians who allow selfish interests to cloud their intelligence, but to give useful hints to such as are bound by the proper oaths to devote their powers to legitimate ends... [3]

LIBER XV, the Mass of the Gnostic Catholic Church

Perhaps Crowley's greatest and most approachable published work of sex magick is *Liber XV, the Mass of the Gnostic Catholic Church*[4] (known commonly as the Gnostic Mass). It is the central ceremony (both public and private) of the O.T.O. and is the ritualized celebration of the Order's supreme secret of magick. That secret emanates from the Sovereign Sanctuary of the Gnosis – the Ninth Degree. It is for all intent and purposes the magical technique that Theodore Ruess initially accused Crowley of revealing.

Sacred and secret as this technique is, Crowley ingeniously crafted his Gnostic Mass to openly communicate and execute the operation in the form of a public ceremony, a shared Eucharist of wine and bread – a dramatic art form that can be witnessed and appreciated by anyone, magician and non-magician alike.) *In beauty is*

---

3 Aleister Crowley, with Mary Desti and Leila Waddell, *Magick—Liber ABA—Book Four*—Part III; Second one-volume edition, revised and enlarged, (York Beach, ME: Weiser Books, 1997). p. 210.
4 Aleister Crowley. *The Equinox III (1) (The Blue Equinox).* Detroit, Spring 1919. Reprint. York Beach, ME: Samuel Weiser, 1992. p. 237.

eternal truth revealed, and the Gnostic Mass is arguably Crowley's most beautiful ritual ceremony.

The Gnostic Mass is very similar in form to the Mass of the Roman Catholic and Eastern Orthodox churches. In fact, Crowley was inspired to create the Mass after attending services at St. Basil's Cathedral[5] in Moscow. As you will see, the most obvious difference between the Crowley's Mass and Christian Masses is the presence of both a Priest and a Priestess. One would correctly assume that the particular sex magick technique the Gnostic Mass deals with is one that is accomplished by one man and one woman. Variations on the theme of this central secret, however, make it also privately amendable for solitary, homosexual and non-sexual workings (Crowley's diaries are full of such experiments). Liber XV, the Gnostic Mass (as written and as officially and publicly celebrated), however, does not reflect or specifically accommodate these other variations in its officers, order of ceremony or formulae.

Anyone who is even slightly familiar with Aleister Crowley and his work knows that he was *not* homophobic. His Gnostic Mass is not a biological, cultural, political or magical statement on the virtues of heterosexual relationships. It is clear to me, however, that Crowley felt that the fundamental essence of this particular magical

---

5 Also known as *Pokrovsky Cathedral*, and the *Cathedral of the Protection of the Most Holy Theotokos on the Moat*, it is the iconic edifice which dominates Moscow's Red Square.

technique could be best first understood, appreciated, and mastered in terms of male/female-lingam/yoni/sperm/egg gender polarities, before experimental variations in the formula are introduced and elaborated upon.

That being said, the formulae of this kind of operation are based on the following postulates:

1. For human beings on the *physical plane*, the supreme creative act is the creation of another living human being.

2. Neither the male *nor* the female of our species is possessed of a full set of human equipment necessary to accomplish this wonder.

3. What is absent in one sex is present in the other.

4. The magical laws that govern the procreative processes which ultimately result in the birth of a physical child are the *same* magical laws that govern creative processes taking place on more subtle planes.

In other words, our physical bodies, male and female, are alchemical laboratories (operating independent of our conscious direction) that routinely transform light and energy from the Sun (from the nutrients we eat) into our tangible flesh, blood, nerves, and brain tissue (and our more intangible aspects such as electrical nerve impulses, magnetic, fields, radiation, light, thought waves, etc.). On the material plan when the male and female elements are joined and combined they are capable of passing our coded essence to a new generation – literally, we can (and regularly *do*) create the living vessel for the incarnating soul of another human being. Used with skill and *full magical intent* the sex magician employs these already-functioning magical 'laboratories' of flesh and blood, nerve, thought, imagination and *will* to create the 'incarnating soul' of whatever object, concept, or level of consciousness her or she might intend to manifest in his or her life.

The focus of this kind of sex magick, is not the physical tools of the operation – it is not the penis or the vagina or the sperm or the egg; it is not the male or the female, father or mother, but in the "child" of their ecstasy – the golden moment of disintegrating ecstatic union when all consciousness of separate existence is dissolved for an eternal instant into the creative bliss of supreme consciousness. In the Gnostic Mass the mother is the Priestess, the father is the Priest and (at the climactic moment) the Child becomes present in the bread and wine that has been charged by the infinite, wall-to-wall radiation that is the result of the ecstatic union of the Priest and Priestess. The host and wine for a golden moment become as it were a living petri dish, an infinitely fertile medium capable of accepting the image (and facilitating the conception) of any thought form a concentrated mind can stamp upon it. Each communicant (each member of the congregation) then has the opportunity to ceremonially consume that child (in the host and wine) and in essence become pregnant with the fertilized object of their own particular heart's desire.

Crowley created Liber XV as a ritual suitable for public celebration, and indeed, because of the international growth of the O.T.O. since Crowley's death it is regularly performed worldwide. It is not obscene or pornographic. Indeed, if it were a movie it would most likely be rated PG (or PG-13 if the Priestess chooses not to resume her robe once the veil is opened). Still, it doesn't take a genius to see the sexual references throughout. Crowley also fantasized a more overtly sexual group ceremony and wrote an account of it in *Liber DCCCXI, Energized Enthusiasm* which was first published in *The Equinox I, 9*. As far as I know the events he describes in this essay are entirely fictional, and represent another attempt for Crowley to be very clear and frank about aspects of sex magick without directly violating his O.T.O. obligations of secrecy. I think you will agree with me that it appears Crowley very much enjoyed playing this literary game of sexual hide and seek.

We've included in this volume a collection of other works that issued from Crowley's pen, but if they were written as literary games they are of a profoundly different order. Indeed, three of them Crowley classified as Class A, "…books of which many be changed not so much as a style of a letter: that is, they represent the utterance of an Adept entirely beyond the criticism of even the Visible Head of the Organization."[6]

---

6 Aleister Crowley, *The Holy Books of Thelema.* (York Beach, ME: Samuel Weiser, 1983), p. 262.

There are thirteen such Class A Libers[7] in all, including *Liber AL vel Legis, The Book of the Law.* The three presented here were first published in *The Equinox I, 6 & 7.* They are:

1. *Liber A'Ash Vel Capricorni Pneumatici Sub Figura CCCLXX*

   - Contains the true secret of all practical magick.[8]

   - The Book of the Creation or of the Goat of the Spirit

   - [A]nalizes the nature of the creative magical force in man, explains how to awaken it, how to use it and indicates the general as well as the particular objects to be gained thereby.[9]

   - The Interpretation of this Book will be given to members of the Grade of Dominus Liminis on application, each to his Adeptus.[10]

   - CCCLXX cu Creation.

2. *Liber Cheth Vel Vallum Abiegni Sub Figura CLVI*

   - This book is a perfect account of the task of Exempt Adept, considered under the symbols of a particular plane, not the intellectual.[11]

---

7 Aleister Crowley, *The Holy Books of Thelema.* (York Beach, ME: Samuel Weiser, 1983), p. xxvii - xxxv.

8 Aleister Crowley, A Syllabus of the Official Instructions of A∴A∴ *The Equinox* I (10), 1913 (reprinted York Beach, ME: Weiser, 1972), pp. 43 – 47.

9 Aleister Crowley, *The Confessions of Aleister Crowley*, (London: Cape, 1969), pp. 673-4.

10 Aleister Crowley, colophon to Liber CCCLXX, *The Equinox* I,6, p. 39.

11 Aleister Crowley, A Syllabus of the Official Instructions of A∴A∴ *The Equinox* I (10), 1913 (reprinted York Beach, ME: Weiser, 1972), pp. 43 – 47.

- The Wall of Abiegnus (the Sacred Mountain of the Rosicrucians) gives the formula of Attainment by devotion to our Lady Babalon. It instructs the aspirant how to dissolve his personality in the Universal Life.[12]

- *CLVI*—Babalon, to whom the book refers. See *Sepher Sephiroth*.[13]

3. *Liber Stellae Rubeae*

- A secret ritual, the Heart of IAO-OAI, delivered unto V.V.V.V.V. for his use in a certain matter of *Liber Legis*, and written down under the figure LCVI.

- This book is sufficiently described by the title.[14]

- *The Book of the Ruby Star*

- [D]escribes an extremely powerful ritual of practical Magick; how to arouse the Magical Force wihin the operator and how to use it to create whatever may be required.[15]

- *LXVI*—The sum of the first 11 numbers. This book relates to Magic, whose Key is 11.[16]

---

12 Aleister Crowley, *The Confessions of Aleister Crowley*, (London: Cape, 1969), pp. 673-4.

13 Aleister Crowley, Syllabus, pp. 53-56.

14 Aleister Crowley, A Syllabus of the Official Instructions of A.·.A.·. *The Equinox* I (10), 1913 (reprinted York Beach, ME: Weiser, 1972), pp. 43 – 47.

15 Aleister Crowley, *The Confessions of Aleister Crowley*, (London: Cape, 1969), pp. 673-4.

16 Aleister Crowley, Syllabus, pp. 53-56.

While not a Class A paper, *Astarte vel Liber Berylli sub figura CLXXV*, which first appeared in *The Equinox I, 7*, is no less a powerful magical document. It is instruction on how the magician unites himself or herself to a particular Deity by means of devotion.

We have also included in this volume, two rituals, also from *The Equinox I, 7, Liber Had*, and *Liber Nu*, which in themselves are not at first glance seen to be rituals of sex magick; but instead are solitary meditations on the two infinities (or primary 'gods') of the Thelemic pantheon; Had (or Hadit), the infinitely contracted center of the cosmos, and Nu (or Nuit) the infinitely expanded circumference of the cosmos.

Because infinite space has no limits, and Nuit is everywhere; therefore the center must also be everywhere. Both the infinitely large infinity and the infinitely small infinity are in infinite contact. This is love making the grandest of scales, But what has all this to do with sex magick? Perhaps easier to ask, "What does sex magick have to do with quantum mechanics? What does space, time, and motion have to do with consciousness?"

For the moment let's just start by pointing out that the Priest in the Gnostic Mass is only the Priest in so much that he can magically embody the cosmic Hadit, and the Priestess is only the Priestess in so much that she can magically embody cosmic Nuit. The union of Nuit and Hadit creates the Child, and the Child is the object of our sex magick operation.

For the bold magician, I strongly advise not only reading and studying *Liber Had* and *Liber Nu*, but practicing and perfecting both of them.

Finally, I would again like to return to *Liber XXXVI, The Star Sapphire*,[17] that tiny work that brought Theodor Reuss to Crowley's door in 1912 and changed his (and mine, and perhaps *your*) life in a most magical way. The Star Sapphire makes reference to "The Holy Hexagram" which can be viewed symbolically as the union of the male (upright) triangle and the female (downturned) triangle. I can't help but speculate that Reuss might have also pointed to Chapter 69 of *The Book of Lies*[18] to further and more explicitly lead the discussion to the sex magick technique he was trying to get Crowley to *discover for himself*. As that particular chapter and its commentary do not later appear anywhere in any of *The Equinox* series I have appended them below for your meditation, your edification, and perhaps—just perhaps—for *your* epiphany.

Lon Milo DuQuette
Costa Mesa, California

---

17 See page 57
18 *Op. cit.* pp. 148-149.

Chapter 69 from *The Book of Lies*

69

ΚΕΦΑΛΗ ΞΘ

THE WAY TO SUCCEED—

AND THE WAY TO SUCK EGGS!

This is the Holy Hexagram.

Plunge from the height, O God, and interlock with Man!

Plunge from the height, O Man, and interlock with Beast!

The Red Triangle is the descending tongue of grace; the Blue Triangle is the ascending tongue of prayer.

This Interchange, the Double Gift of Tongues, the Word of Double Power—**ABRAHADABRA!**—is the sign of the **GREAT WORK**, for the **GREAT WORK** is accomplished in Silence. And behold is not that Word equal to Cheth, that is Cancer, whose Sigil is ♋ ?

This Work also eats up itself, accomplishes its own end, nourishes the worker, leaves no seed, is perfect in itself.

Little children, love one another!

Commentary (ΞΘ)

The key to the understanding of this chapter is given in the number and the title, the former being intelligible to all nations who employ Arabic figures, the latter only to experts in deciphering English puns.

The chapter alludes to Levi's drawing of the Hexagram, and is a criticism of, or improvement upon, it. In the ordinary Hexagram, the Hexagram of nature, the red triangle is upwards, like fire, and the blue triangle downwards, like water. In the magical hexagram this is revered; the descending red triangle is that of Horus, a sign specially revealed by him personally, at the Equinox of the Gods. (It is the flame descending upon the altar, and licking up the burnt offering.) The blue triangle represents the aspiration, since blue is the colour of devotion, and the triangle, kinetically considered, is the symbol of directed force.

In the first three paragraphs this formation of the hexagram is explained; it is a symbol of the mutual separation of the Holy Guardian Angel and his client. In the interlocking is indicated the completion of the work.

Paragraph 4 explains in slightly different language what we have said above, and the scriptural image of tongues is introduced.

In paragraph 5 the symbolism of tongues is further developed. Abrahadabra is our primal example of an interlocked word. We assume that the reader has thoroughly studied that word in Liber D., etc. The sigil of Cancer links up this symbolism with the number of the chapter.

The remaining paragraphs continue the Gallic symbolism.

O.T.O.

LIBER XV

ECCLESIAE GNOSTICAE CATHOLICAE
CANON MISSAE

O. T. O.

Issued by Order:

𝔅𝔞𝔭𝔥𝔬𝔪𝔢𝔱

XI° O. T. O.

HIBERNIAE IONAE ET
OMNIUM BRITANNIARUM
REX SUMMUS SANCTISSIMUS

LIBER XV

O.T.O.

ECCLESIAE GNOSTICAE CATHOLICAE
CANON MISSAE

I

OF THE FURNISHINGS OF THE TEMPLE

In the East, that is, in the direction of Boleskine, which is situated on the South-Eastern shore of Loch Ness in Scotland, two miles east of Foyers, is a shrine or High Altar. Its dimensions should be 7 feet in length, 3 feet in breadth, 44 inches in height. It should be covered with a crimson altar-cloth, on which may be embroidered fleur-de-lys in gold, or a sunblaze, or other suitable emblem.

On each side of it should be a pillar or Obelisk, with countercharges in black and white.

Below it should be the dais of three steps, in black and white squares.

Above it is the super-altar, at whose top is the Stélé of Revealing in reproduction, with four candles on each side of it. Below the stélé is a place for the Book of the Law, with six candles on each side of it. Below this again is The Holy Graal, with roses on each side of it. There is room in front of the Cup for the Paten. On each side beyond the roses, are two great candles.

All this is enclosed within a great Veil.

249

Forming the apex of an equilateral triangle whose base is a line drawn between the pillars, is a small black square altar, of superposed cubes.

Taking this altar as the middle of the base of a similar and equal triangle, at the apex of this second triangle is a small circular font.

Repeating, the apex of a third triangle is an upright Tomb.

II

OF THE OFFICERS OF THE MASS

The PRIEST. Bears the Sacred Lance, and is clothed at first in a plain white robe.

The PRIESTESS. Should be actually Virgo Intacta, or specially dedicated to the service of the Great Order. She is clothed in white, blue, and gold. She bears the Sword from a red girdle, and the Paten and Hosts, or Cakes of Light.

The DEACON. He is clothed in white and yellow. He bears the Book of the Law.

Two Children. They are clothed in white and black. One bears a pitcher of water and a cellar of salt, the other a censer of fire and a casket of perfume.

III

OF THE CEREMONY OF THE INTROIT

The DEACON, *opening the door of the Temple, admits the congregation, and takes his stand between the small altar and the font. (There should be a door-keeper to attend to the admission.)*

The DEACON *advances and bows before the open*

*shrine where the Graal is exalted. He kisses the
Book of the Law three times, opens it, and places
it upon the super-altar. He turns West.*

THE DEACON. Do what thou wilt shall be the whole of the
Law. I proclaim the Law of Light, Life, Love, and Liberty in the name of IAO.

THE CONGREGATION. Love is the law, love under will.

*The DEACON goes to his place between the altar of
incense and the font, faces east, and gives the
step and sign of a Man and a Brother. All imitate
him.*

THE DEACON AND ALL THE PEOPLE. I believe in one secret
and ineffable LORD; and in one Star in the Company of
Stars of whose fire we are created, and to which we shall
return; and in one Father of Life, Mystery of Mystery, in
His name CHAOS, the sole viceregent of the Sun upon the
Earth; and in one Air the nourisher of all that breathes.

And I believe in one Earth, the Mother of us all, and in
one Womb wherein all men are begotten, and wherein they
shall rest, Mystery of Mystery, in Her name BABALON.

And I believe in the Serpent and the Lion, Mystery of
Mystery, in His name BAPHOMET.

And I believe in one Gnostic and Catholic Church of Light,
Life, Love and Liberty, the Word of whose Law is
THELEMA.

And I believe in the communion of Saints.

And, forasmuch as meat and drink are transmuted in us
daily into spiritual substance, I believe in the Miracle of the
Mass.

And I confess one Baptism of Wisdom, whereby we accomplish the Miracle of Incarnation.

251

And I confess my life one, individual, and eternal that was, and is, and is to come.

AUMN. AUMN. AUMN.

> *Music is now played. The child enters with the ewer and the salt. The* VIRGIN *enters with the Sword and the Paten. The child enters with the censer and the perfume. They face the* DEACON, *deploying into line, from the space between the two altars.*

THE VIRGIN. Greeting of Earth and Heaven!

> *All give the Hailing sign of a Magician, the* DEACON *leading.*

> *The* PRIESTESS, *the negative child on her left, the positive on her right, ascends the steps of the High Altar, they awaiting her below. She places the Paten before the Graal. Having adored it, she descends, and with the children following her, the positive next her, she moves in a serpentine manner involving 3½ circles of the temple. (Deosil about altar, widdershins about font, deosil about altar and font, widdershins about altar and to the Tomb in the West.) She draws her Sword, and pulls down the Veil, therewith.*

THE PRIESTESS. By the power of ✠ Iron, I say unto thee, Arise. In the name of our Lord the ✠ Sun, and of our Lord ✠ . . . that thou mayst administer the virtues to the Brethren.

> *She sheathes the Sword.*

> *The* PRIEST, *issuing from the Tomb, holding the Lance erect with both hands, right over left, against his breast, takes the first three regular steps.*

252

He then gives the Lance to the PRIESTESS, *and gives the three penal signs.*

He then kneels, and worships the Lance with both hands.

Penitential music.

THE PRIEST. I am a man among men.

He takes again the Lance, and lowers it. He rises.

THE PRIEST. How should I be worthy to administer the virtues to the Brethren?

The PRIESTESS *takes from the child the water and the salt, and mixes them in the font.*

THE PRIESTESS. Let the salt of Earth admonish the Water to bear the virtue of the Great Sea. (*Genuflects.*) Mother, be thou adored.

She returns to the West. ✠ *on* PRIEST *with open hand doth she make, over his forehead, breast, and body.*

Be the *PRIEST* pure of body and soul!

The PRIESTESS *takes the censer from the child, and places it on the small altar. She puts incense therein.*

Let the Fire and the Air make sweet the world! (*Genuflects.*)

Father, be thou adored.

She returns West, and makes ✠ *with the censer before the* PRIEST, *thrice as before.*

Be the *PRIEST* fervent of body and soul!

(*The children resume their weapons as they are done with.*)

The DEACON *now takes the consecrated Robe from*

the High Altar, and brings it to her. She robes
the PRIEST *in his Robe of scarlet and gold.*

Be the flame of the Sun thine ambience, O thou PRIEST
of the SUN!

The DEACON *brings the crown from the High Altar.*
(*The crown may be of gold or platinum, or of*
electrum magicum; but with no other metals, save
the small proportions necessary to a proper alloy.
It may be adorned with divers jewels, at will. But
it must have the Uraeus serpent twined about it,
and the cap of maintenance must match the scarlet
of the Robe. Its texture should be velvet.)

Be the Serpent thy crown, O thou PRIEST of the LORD!

Kneeling, she takes the Lance, between her open
hands, and runs them up and down upon the shaft
eleven times, very gently.

Be the LORD present among us!

All give the Hailing Sign.

THE PEOPLE. So mote it be.

IV

OF THE CEREMONY OF THE OPENING
OF THE VEIL

THE PRIEST. Thee therefore whom we adore we also invoke.

By the power of the lifted Lance!

He raises the Lance. All repeat Hailing Sign.
A phrase of triumphant music.
The PRIEST *takes the* PRIESTESS *by her right hand*
with his left, keeping the Lance raised.

I, PRIEST and KING, take thee, Virgin pure without

254

spot; I upraise thee; I lead thee to the East; I set thee upon the summit of the Earth.

He thrones the PRIESTESS *upon the altar. The* DEACON *and the children follow, they in rank, behind him.*

The PRIESTESS *takes the Book of the Law, resumes her seat, and holds it open on her breast with her two hands, making a descending triangle with thumbs and forefingers.*

The PRIEST *gives the lance to the* DEACON *to hold, and takes the ewer from the child, and sprinkles the* PRIESTESS, *making five crosses, forehead, shoulders, and thighs.*

The thumb of the PRIEST *is always between his index and medius, whenever he is not holding the Lance.*

The PRIEST *takes the censer from the child, and makes five crosses, as before.*

The children replace their weapons on their respective altars.

The PRIEST *kisses the Book of the Law three times.*

He kneels for a space in adoration, with joined hands, knuckles closed, thumb in position aforesaid.

He rises, and draws the veil over the whole altar.

All rise and stand to order.

The PRIEST *takes the lance from the* DEACON, *and holds it as before, as Osiris or Pthah. He circumambulates the Temple three times, followed by the* DEACON *and the children as before. (These, when not using their hands, keep their arms crossed upon their breasts.)*

255

At the last circumambulation they leave him, and go to the place between the font and the small altar, where they kneel in adoration, their hands joined palm to palm, and raised above their heads.
All imitate this motion.
The PRIEST *returns to the East, and mounts the first step of the altar.*

THE PRIEST.   O circle of Stars whereof our Father is but the younger brother, marvel beyond imagination, soul of infinite space, before whom Time is ashamed, the mind bewildered, and the understanding dark, not unto Thee may we attain, unless Thine image be Love.   Therefore by seed and root and stem and bud and leaf and flower and fruit do we invoke Thee.

Then the priest answered & said unto the Queen of Space, kissing her lovely brows, and the dew of her light bathing his whole body in a sweet-smelling perfume of sweat; O Nuit, continuous one of Heaven, let it be ever thus; that men speak not of thee as One but as None; and let them speak not of thee at all, since thou art continuous.

During this speech the PRIESTESS *must have divested herself completely of her robe.   See CCXX. I. 62.*

THE PRIESTESS.   But to love me is better than all things; if under the night-stars in the desert thou presently burnest mine incense before me, invoking me with a pure heart, and the serpent flame therein, thou shalt come a little to lie in my bosom.   For one kiss wilt thou then be willing to give all; but whoso gives one particle of dust shall lose all in that hour.   Ye shall gather goods and store of women and spices; ye shall wear rich jewels; ye shall exceed the nations of earth in splendour and pride; but always in the love of

256

me, and so shall ye come to my joy. I charge you earnestly to come before me in a single robe, and covered with a rich head-dress. I love you! I yearn to you! Pale or purple, veiled or voluptuous, I who am all pleasure and purple, and drunkenness of the innermost sense, desire you. Put on the wings, and arouse the coiled splendour within you: come unto me! To me! To me! Sing the rapturous love-song unto me! Burn to me perfumes! Drink to me, for I love you! I love you. I am the blue-lidded daughter of sunset; I am the naked brilliance of the voluptuous night-sky. To me! To me!

The PRIEST *mounts the second step.*

THE PRIEST. O secret of secrets that art hidden in the being of all that lives, not Thee do we adore, for that which adoreth is also Thou. Thou art That, and That am I.

I am the flame that burns in every heart of man, and in the core of every star. I am Life, and the giver of Life; yet therefore is the knowledge of me the knowledge of death. I am alone; there is no God where I am.

The DEACON *and all rise to their feet, with the Hailing sign.*

THE DEACON. But ye, O my people, rise up and awake.

Let the rituals be rightly performed with joy and beauty.

There are rituals of the elements and feasts of the times.

A feast for the first night of the Prophet and his Bride.

A feast for the three days of the writing of the Book of the Law.

A feast for Tahuti and the children of the Prophet—secret, O Prophet!

A feast for the Supreme Ritual, and a feast for the Equinox of the Gods.

257

A feast for fire and a feast for water; a feast for life and a greater feast for death.

A feast every day in your hearts in the joy of my rapture.

A feast every night unto Nu, and the pleasure of uttermost delight.

The PRIEST *mounts the third step.*

THE PRIEST. Thou that art One, our Lord in the Universe the Sun, our Lord in ourselves whose name is Mystery of Mystery, uttermost being whose radiance enlightening the worlds is also the breath that maketh every God even and Death to tremble before Thee—By the Sign of Light ✠ appear Thou glorious upon the throne of the Sun.

Make open the path of creation and of intelligence between us and our minds. Enlighten our understanding.

Encourage our hearts. Let thy light crystallize itself in our blood, fulfilling us of Resurrection.

A ka dua

Tuf ur biu

bi a'a chefu

Dudu nur af an nuteru.

THE PRIESTESS. There is no law beyond Do what thou wilt.

The PRIEST *parts the veil with his lance. During the previous speeches the* PRIESTESS *has, if necessary, as in savage countries, resumed her robe.*

THE PRIEST. IO IO IO IAO SABAO KURIE ABRASAX KURIE MEITHRAS KURIE PHALLE. IO PAN IO PAN PAN IO ISCHURON IO ATHANATON IO ABROTON IO IAO. CHAIRE PHALLE CHAIRE PAMPHAGE CHAIRE PANGENETOR. HAGIOS HAGIOS HAGIOS IAO.

258

ECCLESIAE GNOSTICAE CATHOLICAE

The PRIESTESS *is seated with the Paten in her right hand and the cup in her left.*

The PRIEST *presents the Lance, which she kisses eleven times. She then holds it to her breast, while the* PRIEST, *falling at her knees, kisses them, his arms stretched along her thighs. He remains in this adoration while the Deacon intones the collects.*

All stand to order, with the Dieu Garde, that is, feet square, hands, with linked thumbs, held loosely. This is the universal position when standing, unless other direction is given.

V

OF THE OFFICE OF THE COLLECTS, WHICH ARE ELEVEN IN NUMBER

(THE SUN)

THE DEACON. Lord visible and sensible of whom this earth is but a frozen spark turning about thee with annual and diurnal motion, source of light, source of life, let thy perpetual radiance hearten us to continual labour and enjoyment; so that as we are constant partakers of thy bounty we may in our particular orbit give out light and life, sustenance and joy to them that revolve about us without diminution of substance or effulgence for ever.

THE PEOPLE. So mote it be.

(THE LORD)

THE DEACON. Lord secret and most holy, source of life, source of love, source of liberty, be thou ever constant and

259

mighty within us, force of energy, fire of motion; with diligence let us ever labour with thee, that we may remain in thine abundant joy.

THE PEOPLE. So mote it be.

(THE MOON)

THE DEACON. Lady of night, that turning ever about us art now visible and now invisible in thy season, be thou favourable to hunters, and lovers, and to all men that toil upon the earth, and to all mariners upon the sea.

THE PEOPLE. So mote it be.

(THE LADY)

THE DEACON. Giver and receiver of joy, gate of life and love, be thou ever ready, thou and thine handmaiden, in thine office of gladness.

THE PEOPLE. So mote it be.

(THE SAINTS)

THE DEACON. Lord of Life and Joy, that art the might of man, that art the essence of every true god that is upon the surface of the Earth, continuing knowledge from generation unto generation, thou adored of us upon heaths and in woods, on mountains and in caves, openly in the marketplaces and secretly in the chambers of our houses, in temples of gold and ivory and marble as in these other temples of our bodies, we worthily commemorate them worthy that did of old adore thee and manifest thy glory unto men, *Laotze and Siddartha* and Krishna *and Tahuti,* Mosheh, *Dionysus, Mohammed and To Mega Therion, with these also* Hermes, *Pan,* Priapus, Osiris and Melchizedek, *Khem* and Amoun *and Mentu,* Heracles, Orpheus and Odysseus; with Vergilius, *Catullus,* Martialis, *Rabelais, Swinburne, and many*

260

ECCLESIAE GNOSTICAE CATHOLICAE

an holy bard; Apollonius Tyanaeus, Simon Magus, Manes, Basilides, Valentinus, *Bardesanes and Hippolytus, that transmitted the Light of the Gnosis to us their successors and their heirs;* with Merlin, Arthur, Kamuret, Parzival, and many another, prophet, priest and king, that bore the Lance and Cup, the Sword and Disk, against the Heathen; *and these also,* Carolus Magnus and his paladins, with William of Schyren, Frederick of Hohenstaufen, Roger Bacon, *Jacobus Burgundus Molensis the Martyr, Christian Rosencreutz,* Ulrich von Hutten, Paracelsus, Michael Maier, Jacob Boehme, Francis Bacon Lord Verulam, Andrea, Robertus de Fluctibus, Johannes Dee, *Sir Edward Kelly,* Thomas Vaughan, Elias Ashmole, Molinos, Wolfgang von Goethe, Ludovicus Rex Bavariæ, Richard Wagner, *Alphonse Louis Constant,* Friedrich Nietzsche, Hargrave Jennings, Carl Kellner, Forlong dux, Sir Richard Payne Knight, Sir Richard Francis Burton, Doctor Gérard Encausse, *Doctor Theodor Reuss, and Sir Aleister Crowley—*oh Sons of the Lion and the Snake! with all Thy saints we worthily commemorate them worthy that were and are and are to come.

May their Essence be here present, potent, puissant and paternal to perfect this feast!

    (At each name the DEACON *signs* ✠ *with thumb between index and medius. At ordinary mass it is only necessary to commemorate those whose names are italicized, with wording as is shown.)*

THE PEOPLE. So mote it be.

(THE EARTH)

THE DEACON. Mother of fertility on whose breast lieth water, whose cheek is caressed by air, and in whose heart

261

is the sun's fire, womb of all life, recurring grace of seasons, answer favourably the prayer of labour, and to pastors and husbandmen be thou propitious.

THE PEOPLE. So mote it be.

(THE PRINCIPLES)

THE DEACON. Mysterious Energy, triform, mysterious Matter, in fourfold and sevenfold division, the interplay of which things weave the dance of the Veil of Life upon the Face of the Spirit, let there be Harmony and Beauty in your mystic loves, that in us may be health and wealth and strength and divine pleasure according to the Law of Liberty; let each pursue his Will as a strong man that rejoiceth in his way, as the course of a Star that blazeth for ever among the joyous company of Heaven.

THE PEOPLE. So mote it be.

(BIRTH)

THE DEACON. Be the hour auspicious, and the gate of life open in peace and in well-being, so that she that beareth children may rejoice, and the babe catch life with both hands.

THE PEOPLE. So mote it be.

(MARRIAGE)

THE DEACON. Upon all that this day unite with love under will let fall success; may strength and skill unite to bring forth ecstasy, and beauty answer beauty.

THE PEOPLE. So mote it be.

(DEATH)

THE DEACON. Term of all that liveth, whose name is inscrutable, be favourable unto us in thine hour.

THE PEOPLE. So mote it be.

ECCLESIAE GNOSTICAE CATHOLICAE

THE DEACON. Unto them from whose eyes the veil of life hath fallen may there be granted the accomplishment of their true Wills; whether they will absorption in the Infinite, or to be united with their chosen and preferred, or to be in contemplation, or to be at peace, or to achieve the labour and heroism of incarnation on this planet or another, or in any Star, or aught else, unto them may there be granted the accomplishment of their wills; yea, the accomplishment of their wills. AUMN. AUMN. AUMN.

THE PEOPLE. So mote it be.

All sit.

> *The* DEACON *and the children attend the* PRIEST *and* PRIESTESS, *ready to hold any appropriate weapon as may be necessary.*

VI

OF THE CONSECRATION OF THE ELEMENTS

The PRIEST *makes the five crosses.* ✠1 *on paten*
✠3 ✠2
and cup; ✠4 *on paten alone;* ✠5 *on cup alone.*

THE PRIEST. Life of man upon earth, fruit of labour, sustenance of endeavour, thus be thou nourishment of the Spirit!

> *He touches the Host with the Lance.*

By the virtue of the Rod
Be this bread the Body of God!

> *He takes the Host.*

TOUTO ESTI TO SŌMA MOU.

263

He kneels, adores, rises, turns, shows Host to the
PEOPLE, *turns, replaces Host, and adores.* Music.
He takes the Cup.

Vehicle of the joy of Man upon earth, solace of labour, inspiration of endeavour, thus be thou ecstasy of the Spirit!

He touches the Cup with the Lance.

By the virtue of the Rod
Be this wine the Blood of God!

He takes the Cup.

TOUTO ECTI TO ΠOTHPION
TOU HAIMATOC MOU.

He kneels, adores, rises, turns, shows the Cup to the
PEOPLE, *turns, replaces the Cup, and adores.* Music.

For this is the Covenant of Resurrection.

He makes the five crosses on the PRIESTESS.

Accept, O LORD, this sacrifice of life and joy, true warrants of the Covenant of Resurrection.

The PRIEST *offers the Lance to the* PRIESTESS, *who kisses it; he then touches her between the breasts and upon the body. He then flings out his arms upward, as comprehending the whole shrine.*

Let this offering be borne upon the waves of Æthyr to our Lord and Father the Sun that travelleth over the Heavens in his name ON.

He closes his hands, kisses the PRIESTESS *between the breasts, and makes three great crosses over the Paten, the Cup, and himself.*

He strikes his breast. All repeat this action.

Hear ye all, saints of the true church of old time now essentially present, that of ye we claim heirship, with ye we claim communion, from ye we claim benediction in the name of IAO.

264

ECCLESIAE GNOSTICAE CATHOLICAE

He makes three crosses on Paten and Cup together.
He uncovers the Cup, genuflects, takes the Cup in his
left hand and the Host in his right.
With the Host he makes the five crosses on the Cup.

✠1

✠3　　✠2

✠5 ✠4

He elevates the Host and the Cup.
The Bell strikes.
HAGIOS HAGIOS HAGIOS IAO.
He replaces the Host and the Cup, and adores.

VII

OF THE OFFICE OF THE ANTHEM.

THE PRIEST.　Thou who art I, beyond all I am,
Who hast no nature and no name,
Who art, when all but thou are gone,
Thou, centre and secret of the Sun,
Thou, hidden spring of all things known
And unknown, Thou aloof, alone,
Thou, the true fire within the seed
Brooding and breeding, source and seed
Of life, love, liberty, and light,
Thou beyond speech and beyond sight,
Thee I invoke, my faint fresh fire
Kindling as mine intents aspire.
Thee I invoke, abiding one,
Thee, centre and secret of the Sun,
And that most holy mystery
Of which the vehicle am I.

265

Appear, most awful and most mild,
As it is lawful, to thy child!
THE CHORUS. For of the Father and the Son
The Holy Spirit is the norm;
Male-female, quintessential, one,
Man-being veiled in woman-form.
Glory and worship in the highest,
Thou Dove, mankind that deifiest,
Being that race, most royally run
To spring sunshine through winter storm.
Glory and worship be to Thee,
Sap of the world-ash, wonder-tree!
FIRST SEMICHORUS. MEN. Glory to thee from gilded tomb!
SECOND SEMICHORUS. WOMEN. Glory to thee from waiting womb!
MEN. Glory to Thee from earth unploughed!
WOMEN. Glory to Thee from virgin vowed!
MEN. Glory to Thee, true Unity
Of the eternal Trinity!
WOMEN. Glory to Thee, thou sire and dam
And self of I am that I am!
MEN. Glory to Thee, beyond all term,
Thy spring of sperm, thy seed and germ!
WOMEN. Glory to Thee, eternal Sun,
Thou One in Three, Thou Three in One!
CHORUS. Glory and worship unto Thee,
Sap of the world-ash, wonder-tree!

> *(These words are to form the substance of the an-*
> *them; but the whole or any part thereof shall be*
> *set to music, which may be as elaborate as art can*
> *devise. But even should other anthems be au-*

266

ECCLESIAE GNOSTICAE CATHOLICAE

thorized by the Father of the Church, this shall hold its place as the first of its kind, the father of all others.)

VIII

OF THE MYSTIC MARRIAGE AND CONSUM- MATION OF THE ELEMENTS

The PRIEST *takes the Paten between the index and medius of the right hand. The* PRIESTESS *clasps the Cup in her right hand.*

THE PRIEST. Lord most secret, bless this spiritual food unto our bodies, bestowing upon us health and wealth and strength and joy and peace, and that fulfilment of will and of love under will that is perpetual happiness.

He makes ✠ with Paten and kisses it.
He uncovers the Cup, genuflects, rises.   Music.
He takes the Host, and breaks it over the Cup.
He replaces the right-hand portion in the Paten.
He breaks off a particle of the left-hand portion.

TOUTO ECTI TO ΣΠΕΡΜΑ MOU.   HO ΠΑΤΗΡ ECTIN HO HUIOC DIA TO ΠΝΕΥΜΑ HAGION. AUMN.   AUMN.   AUMN.

He replaces the left-hand part of the Host.
The PRIESTESS *extends the Lance-point with her left hand to receive the particle.*
The PRIEST *clasps the Cup in his left hand.*
Together they depress the Lance-point in the Cup.

THE PRIEST AND THE PRIESTESS.   HRILIU.

The PRIEST *takes the Lance.*
The PRIESTESS *covers the Cup.*

267

The PRIEST *genuflects, rises, bows, joins hands.*
He strikes his breast.

THE PRIEST.   O Lion and O Serpent that destroy the destroyer, be mighty among us.

O Lion and O Serpent that destroy the destroyer, be mighty among us.

O Lion and O Serpent that destroy the destroyer, be mighty among us.

The PRIEST *joins hands upon the breast of the* PRIESTESS, *and takes back his Lance.*

He turns to the PEOPLE, *lowers and raises the Lance, and makes* ✠ *upon them.*

Do what thou wilt shall be the whole of the Law.

THE PEOPLE.   Love is the law, love under will.

He lowers the Lance, and turns to East.

The PRIESTESS *takes the Lance in her right hand.*

With her left hand she offers the Paten.

The PRIEST *kneels.*

THE PRIEST.   In my mouth be the essence of the life of the Sun!

He takes the Host with the right hand, makes ✠ *with it on the Paten, and consumes it.*

Silence.

The PRIESTESS *takes, uncovers, and offers the Cup, as before.*

THE PRIEST.   In my mouth be the essence of the joy of the earth!

He takes the Cup, makes ✠ *on the* PRIESTESS, *drains it and returns it.*

Silence.

268

ECCLESIAE GNOSTICAE CATHOLICAE

He rises, takes the Lance, and turns to the PEOPLE.

THE PRIEST. There is no part of me that is not of the Gods.

(Those of the PEOPLE *who intend to communicate, and none other should be present, having signified their intention, a whole Cake of Light, and a whole goblet of wine, have been prepared for each one. The* DEACON *marshals them; they advance one by one to the altar. The children take the Elements and offer them. The* PEOPLE *communicate as did the* PRIEST, *uttering the same words in an attitude of Resurrection: There is no part of me that is not of the Gods.*

The exceptions to this part of the ceremony are when it is of the nature of a celebration, in which case none but the PRIEST *communicate; or part of the ceremony of marriage, when none other, save the two to be married, partake; part of the ceremony of baptism, when only the child baptised partakes; and of Confirmation at puberty, when only the persons confirmed partake. The Sacrament may be reserved by the* PRIEST, *for administration to the sick in their homes.)*

The PRIEST *closes all within the veil. With the Lance he makes* ✠ *on the people thrice, thus.*

THE PRIEST.✠ The LORD bless you.

✠The LORD enlighten your minds and comfort your hearts and sustain your bodies.

✠The LORD bring you to the accomplishment of your true Wills, the Great Work, the Summum Bonum, True Wisdom and Perfect Happiness.

269

He goes out, the DEACON *and children following, into
the Tomb of the West.*

Music. (*Voluntary.*)

NOTE. *The Priestess and other officers never partake
of the Sacrament, they being as it were part of the*
PRIEST *himself.*

NOTE. *Certain secret Formulae of this Mass are
taught to the* PRIEST *in his Ordination.*

270

ENERGIZED ENTHUSIASM

ENERGIZED ENTHUSIASM

A NOTE ON THEURGY

I

I A O the supreme One of the Gnostics, the true God, is the Lord of this work. Let us therefore invoke Him by that name which the Companions of the Royal Arch blaspheme to aid us in the essay to declare the means which He has bestowed upon us !

II

The divine consciousness which is reflected and refracted in the works of Genius feeds upon a certain secretion, as I believe. This secretion is analogous to semen, but not identical with it. There are but few men and fewer women, those women being invariably androgyne, who possess it at any time in any quantity.

So closely is this secretion connected with the sexual economy that it appears to me at times as if it might be a by-product of that process which generates semen. That some form of this doctrine has been generally accepted is shown in the prohibitions of all religions. Sanctity has been assumed to depend on chastity, and chastity has nearly always been interpreted as abstinence. But I doubt whether the relation is so simple as this would imply ; for example, I

19

find in myself that manifestations of mental creative force always concur with some abnormal condition of the physical powers of generation. But it is not the case that long periods of chastity, on the one hand, or excess of orgies, on the other, are favourable to its manifestation or even to its formation.

I know myself, and in me it is extremely strong; its results are astounding.

For example, I wrote *Tannhäuser*, complete from conception to execution, in sixty-seven consecutive hours. I was unconscious of the fall of nights and days, even after stopping; nor was there any reaction of fatigue. This work was written when I was twenty-four years old, immediately on the completion of an orgie which would normally have tired me out.

Often and often have I noticed that sexual satisfaction so-called has left me dissatisfied and unfatigued, and let loose the floods of verse which have disgraced my career.

Yet, on the contrary, a period of chastity has sometimes fortified me for a great outburst. This is far from being invariably the case. At the conclusion of the K 2 expedition, after five months of chastity, I did no work whatever, barring very few odd lyrics, for months afterwards.

I may mention the year 1911. At this time I was living, in excellent good health, with the woman whom I loved. Her health was, however, variable, and we were both constantly worried.

The weather was continuously fine and hot. For a period of about three months I hardly missed a morning; always on waking I burst out with a new idea which had to be written down.

20

ENERGIZED ENTHUSIASM

The total energy of my being was very high. My weight was 10 stone 8 lb., which had been my fighting weight when I was ten years younger. We walked some twenty miles daily through hilly forest.

The actual amount of MSS. written at this time is astounding; their variety is even more so; of their excellence I will not speak.

Here is a rough list from memory; it is far from exhaustive:

(1) Some dozen books of A ∴ A ∴ instruction, including Liber Astarte, and the Temple of Solomon the King for *Equinox VII*.

(2) Short Stories: The Woodcutter.
His Secret Sin.

(3) Plays: His Majesty's Fiddler
Elder Eel
Adonis ⎫ written straight off, one
The Ghouls ⎭ after the other
Mortadello.

(4) Poems: The Sevenfold Sacrament
A Birthday.

(5) Fundamentals of the Greek Qabalah (involving the collection and analysis of several thousand words).

I think this phenomenon is unique in the history of literature.

I may further refer to my second journey to Algeria, where my sexual life, though fairly full, had been unsatisfactory.

On quitting Biskra, I was so full of ideas that I had to get off the train at El-Kantara, where I wrote " The Scorpion." Five or six poems were written on the way to Paris; " The

21

Ordeal of Ida Pendragon" during my twenty-four hours' stay in Paris, and "Snowstorm" and "The Electric Silence" immediately on my return to England.

To sum up, I can always trace a connection between my sexual condition and the condition of artistic creation, which is so close as to approach identity, and yet so loose that I cannot predicate a single important proposition.

It is these considerations which give me pain when I am reproached by the ignorant with wishing to produce genius mechanically. I may fail, but my failure is a thousand times greater than their utmost success.

I shall therefore base my remarks not so much on the observations which I have myself made, and the experiments which I have tried, as on the accepted classical methods of producing that energized enthusiasm which is the lever that moves God.

III

The Greeks say that there are three methods of discharging the genial secretion of which I have spoken. They thought perhaps that their methods tended to secrete it, but this I do not believe altogether, or without a qualm. For the manifestation of force implies force, and this force must have come from somewhere. Easier I find it to say "subconsciousness" and "secretion" than to postulate an external reservoir, to extend my connotation of "man" than to invent "God."

However, parsimony apart, I find it in my experience that it is useless to flog a tired horse. There are times when I am absolutely bereft of even one drop of this elixir. Nothing

22

ENERGIZED ENTHUSIASM

will restore it, neither rest in bed, nor drugs, nor exercise.
On the other hand, sometimes when after a severe spell of
work I have been dropping with physical fatigue, perhaps
sprawling on the floor, too tired to move hand or foot, the
occurrence of an idea has restored me to perfect intensity of
energy, and the working out of the idea has actually got rid
of the aforesaid physical fatigue, although it involved a great
additional labour.

Exactly parallel (nowhere meeting) is the case of mania.
A madman may struggle against six trained athletes for
hours, and show no sign of fatigue. Then he will suddenly
collapse, but at a second's notice from the irritable idea will
resume the struggle as fresh as ever. Until we discovered
"unconscious muscular action" and its effects, it was rational
to suppose such a man "possessed of a devil"; and the
difference between the madman and the genius is not in the
quantity but in the quality of their work. Genius is organized, madness chaotic. Often the organization of genius is on
original lines, and ill-balanced and ignorant medicine-men
mistake it for disorder. Time has shown that Whistler and
Gauguin "kept rules" as well as the masters whom they were
supposed to be upsetting.

IV

The Greeks say that there are three methods of discharging
the Leyden Jar of Genius. These three methods they assign
to three Gods.

These three Gods are Dionysus, Apollo, Aphrodite. In
English: wine, woman and song.

Now it would be a great mistake to imagine that the

23

Greeks were recommending a visit to a brothel. As well condemn the High Mass at St. Peter's on the strength of having witnessed a Protestant revival meeting. Disorder is always a parody of order, because there is no archetypal disorder that it might resemble. Owen Seaman can parody a poet; nobody can parody Owen Seaman. A critic is a bundle of impressions; there is no ego behind it. All photographs are essentially alike; the works of all good painters essentially differ.

Some writers suppose that in the ancient rites of Eleusis the High Priest publicly copulated with the High Priestess. Were this so, it would be no more "indecent" than it is "blasphemous" for the priest to make bread and wine into the body and blood of God.

True, the Protestants say that it is blasphemous; but a Protestant is one to whom all things sacred are profane, whose mind being all filth can see nothing in the sexual act but a crime or a jest, whose only facial gestures are the sneer and the leer.

Protestantism is the excrement of human thought, and accordingly in Protestant countries art, if it exist at all, only exists to revolt. Let us return from this unsavoury allusion to our consideration of the methods of the Greeks.

V

Agree then that it does not follow from the fact that wine, woman and song make the sailor's tavern that these ingredients must necessarily concoct a hell-broth.

There are some people so simple as to think that, when

24

they have proved the religious instinct to be a mere efflorescence of the sex-instinct, they have destroyed religion.

We should rather consider that the sailor's tavern gives him his only glimpse of heaven, just as the destructive criticism of the phallicists has only proved sex to be a sacrament. Consciousness, says the materialist, axe in hand, is a function of the brain. He has only re-formulated the old saying, " Your bodies are the temples of the Holy Ghost." I

Now sex is justly hallowed in this sense, that it is the eternal fire of the race. Huxley admitted that "some of the lower animalculæ are in a sense immortal," because they go on reproducing eternally by fission, and however often you divide x by 2 there is always something left. But he never seems to have seen that mankind is immortal in exactly the same sense, and goes on reproducing itself with similar characteristics through the ages, changed by circumstance indeed, but always identical in itself. But the spiritual flower of this process is that at the moment of discharge a physical ecstasy occurs, a spasm analogous to the mental spasm which meditation gives. And further, in the sacramental and ceremonial use of the sexual act, the divine consciousness may be attained.

VI

The sexual act being then a sacrament, it remains to consider in what respect this limits the employment of the organs.

First, it is obviously legitimate to employ them for their natural physical purpose. But if it be allowable to use them

25

ceremonially for a religious purpose, we shall find the act hedged about with many restrictions.

For in this case the organs become holy. It matters little to mere propagation that men should be vicious; the most debauched roué might and almost certainly would beget more healthy children than a semi-sexed prude. So the so-called "moral" restraints are not based on reason; thus they are neglected.

But admit its religious function, and one may at once lay down that the act must not be profaned. It must not be undertaken lightly and foolishly without excuse.

It may be undertaken for the direct object of continuing the race.

It may be undertaken in obedience to real passion; for passion, as its name implies, is rather inspired by a force of divine strength and beauty without the will of the individual, often even against it.

It is the casual or habitual—what Christ called "idle"—use or rather abuse of these forces which constitutes their profanation. It will further be obvious that, if the act in itself is to be the sacrament in a religious ceremony, this act must be accomplished solely for the love of God. All personal considerations must be banished utterly. Just as any priest can perform the miracle of transubstantiation, so can any man, possessing the necessary qualifications, perform this other miracle, whose nature must form the subject of a subsequent discussion.

Personal aims being destroyed, it is *à fortiori* necessary to neglect social and other similar considerations.

Physical strength and beauty are necessary and desirable

26

for æsthetic reasons, the attention of the worshippers being liable to distraction if the celebrants are ugly, deformed, or incompetent. I need hardly emphasize the necessity for the strictest self-control and concentration on their part. As it would be blasphemy to enjoy the gross taste of the wine of the sacrament, so must the celebrant suppress even the minutest manifestation of animal pleasure.

Of the qualifying tests there is no necessity to speak ; it is sufficient to say that the adepts have always known how to secure efficiency.

Needless also to insist on a similar quality in the assistants ; the sexual excitement must be suppressed and transformed into its religious equivalent.

VII

With these preliminaries settled in order to guard against foreseen criticisms of those Protestants who, God having made them a little lower than the Angels, have made themselves a great deal lower than the beasts by their consistently bestial interpretation of all things human and divine, we may consider first the triune nature of these ancient methods of energizing enthusiasm.

Music has two parts ; tone or pitch, and rhythm. The latter quality associates it with the dance, and that part of dancing which is not rhythm is sex. Now that part of sex which is not a form of the dance, animal movement, is intoxication of the soul, which connects it with wine. Further identities will suggest themselves to the student.

27

By the use of the three methods in one the whole being of man may thus be stimulated.

The music will create a general harmony of the brain, leading it in its own paths ; the wine affords a general stimulus of the animal nature ; and the sex-excitement elevates the moral nature of the man by its close analogy with the highest ecstasy. It remains, however, always for him to make the final transmutation. Unless he have the special secretion which I have postulated, the result will be commonplace.

So consonant is this system with the nature of man that it is exactly parodied and profaned not only in the sailor's tavern, but in the Society ball. Here, for the lowest natures the result is drunkenness, disease and death ; for the middle natures a gradual blunting of the finer feelings ; for the higher, an exhilaration amounting at the best to the foundation of a life-long love.

If these Society "rites" are properly performed, there should be no exhaustion. After a ball, one should feel the need of a long walk in the young morning air. The weariness or boredom, the headache or somnolence, are Nature's warnings.

VIII

Now the purpose of such a ball, the moral attitude on entering, seems to me to be of supreme importance. If you go with the idea of killing time, you are rather killing yourself. Baudelaire speaks of the first period of love when the boy kisses the trees of the wood, rather than kiss nothing. At the age of thirty-six I found myself at Pompeii, passionately

28

kissing that great grave statue of a woman that stands in the avenue of the tombs. Even now, as I wake in the morning, I sometimes fall to kissing my own arms.

It is with such a feeling that one should go to a ball, and with such a feeling intensified, purified and exalted, that one should leave it.

If this be so, how much more if one go with the direct religious purpose burning in one's whole being! Beethoven roaring at the sunrise is no strange spectacle to me, who shout with joy and wonder, when I understand (without which one cannot really be said ever to see) a blade of grass. I fall upon my knees in speechless adoration at the moon ; I hide my eyes in holy awe from a good Van Gogh.

Imagine then a ball in which the music is the choir celestial, the wine the wine of the Graal, or that of the Sabbath of the Adepts, and one's partner the Infinite and Eternal One, the True and Living God Most High!

Go even to a common ball—the Moulin de la Galette will serve even the least of my magicians—with your whole soul aflame within you, and your whole will concentrated on these transubstantiations, and tell me what miracle takes place!

It is the hate of, the distaste for, life that sends one to the ball when one is old ; when one is young one is on springs until the hour falls ; but the love of God, which is the only true love, diminishes not with age ; it grows deeper and intenser with every satisfaction. It seems as if in the noblest men this secretion constantly increases—which certainly suggests an external reservoir—so that age loses all its bitterness. We find " Brother Lawrence," Nicholas Herman of Lorraine, at the age of eighty in continuous enjoyment of

29

union with God. Buddha at an equal age would run up and down the Eight High Trances like an acrobat on a ladder; stories not too dissimilar are told of Bishop Berkeley. Many persons have not attained union at all until middle age, and then have rarely lost it.

It is true that genius in the ordinary sense of the word has nearly always showed itself in the young. Perhaps we should regard such cases as Nicholas Herman as cases of acquired genius..

Now I am certainly of opinion that genius can be acquired, or, in the alternative, that it is an almost universal possession. Its rarity may be attributed to the crushing influence of a corrupted society. It is rare to meet a youth without high ideals, generous thoughts, a sense of holiness, of his own importance, which, being interpreted, is, of his own identity with God. Three years in the world, and he is a bank clerk or even a government official. Only those who intuitively understand from early boyhood that they must stand out, and who have the incredible courage and endurance to do so in face of all that tyranny, callousness, and the scorn of inferiors can do; only these arrive at manhood uncontaminated.

Every serious or spiritual thought is made a jest; poets are thought "soft" and "cowardly," apparently because they are the only boys with a will of their own and courage to hold out against the whole school, boys and masters in league as once were Pilate and Herod; honour is replaced by expediency, holiness by hypocrisy.

Even where we find thoroughly good seed sprouting in favourable ground, too often is there a frittering away of the forces. Facile encouragement of a poet or painter is far
30

worse for him than any amount of opposition. Here again the sex question (S.Q. so-called by Tolstoyans, chastity-mongers, nut-fooders, and such who talk and think of nothing else) intrudes its horrid head. I believe that every boy is originally conscious of sex as sacred. But he does not know what it is. With infinite diffidence he asks. The master replies with holy horror ; the boy with a low leer, a furtive laugh, perhaps worse.

I am inclined to agree with the Head Master of Eton that pæderastic passions among schoolboys "do no harm"; further, I think them the only redeeming feature of sexual life at public schools.

The Hindoos are wiser. At the well-watched hour of puberty the boy is prepared as for a sacrament ; he is led to a duly consecrated temple, and there by a wise and holy woman, skilled in the art, and devoted to this end, he is initiated with all solemnity into the mystery of life.

The act is thus declared religious, sacred, impersonal, utterly apart from amorism and eroticism and animalism and sentimentalism and all the other vilenesses that Protestantism has made of it.

The Catholic Church did, I believe, to some extent preserve the Pagan tradition. Marriage is a sacrament.[1] But in the attempt to deprive the act of all accretions which would profane it, the Fathers of the Church added in spite of themselves other accretions which profaned it more. They tied it to property and inheritance. They wished it to serve both God and Mammon.

[1] Of course there has been a school of devilish ananders that has held the act in itself to be " wicked." Of such blasphemers of Nature let no further word be said.

31

Rightly restraining the priest, who should employ his whole energy in the miracle of the Mass, they found their counsel a counsel of perfection. The magical tradition was in part lost; the priest could not do what was expected of him, and the unexpended portion of his energy turned sour.

Hence the thoughts of priests, like the thoughts of modern faddists, revolved eternally around the S.Q.

A special and Secret Mass, a Mass of the Holy Ghost, a Mass of the Mystery of the Incarnation, to be performed at stated intervals, might have saved both monks and nuns, and given the Church eternal dominion of the world.

IX

To return. The rarity of genius is in great part due to the destruction of its young. Even as in physical life that is a favoured plant one of whose thousand seeds ever shoots forth a blade, so do conditions kill all but the strongest sons of genius.

But just as rabbits increased apace in Australia, where even a missionary has been known to beget ninety children in two years, so shall we be able to breed genius if we can find the conditions which hamper it, and remove them.

The obvious practical step to take is to restore the rites of Bacchus, Aphrodite and Apollo to their proper place. They should not be open to every one, and manhood should be the reward of ordeal and initiation.

The physical tests should be severe, and weaklings should be killed out rather than artificially preserved. The same remark applies to intellectual tests. But such tests should be as wide as possible. I was an absolute duffer at school in all

32

forms of athletics and games, because I despised them. I held, and still hold, numerous mountaineering world's records. Similarly, examinations fail to test intelligence. Cecil Rhodes refused to employ any man with a University degree. That such degrees lead to honour in England is a sign of England's decay, though even in England they are usually the stepping-stones to clerical idleness or pedagogic slavery.

Such is a dotted outline of the picture that I wish to draw. If the power to possess property depended on a man's competence, and his perception of real values, a new aristocracy would at once be created, and the deadly fact that social consideration varies with the power of purchasing champagne would cease to be a fact. Our pluto-hetairo-politicocracy would fall in a day.

But I am only too well aware that such a picture is not likely to be painted. We can then only work patiently and in secret. We must select suitable material and train it in utmost reverence to these three master-methods, or aiding the soul in its genial orgasm.

X

This reverent attitude is of an importance which I cannot over-rate. Normal people find normal relief from any general or special excitement in the sexual act.

Commander Marston, R.N., whose experiments in the effect of the tom-tom on the married Englishwoman are classical and conclusive, has admirably described how the vague unrest which she at first shows gradually assumes the sexual form, and culminates, if allowed to do so, in shameless masturbation or indecent advances. But this is a natural

33

corollary of the proposition that married Englishwomen are usually unacquainted with sexual satisfaction. Their desires are constantly stimulated by brutal and ignorant husbands, and never gratified. This fact again accounts for the amazing prevalence of Sapphism in London Society.

The Hindus warn their pupils against the dangers of breathing exercises. Indeed the slightest laxness in moral or physical tissues may cause the energy accumulated by the practice to discharge itself by involuntary emission. I have known this happen in my own experience.

It is then of the utmost importance to realize that the relief of the tension is to be found in what the Hebrews and the Greeks called prophesying, and which is better when organized into art. The disorderly discharge is mere waste, a wilderness of howlings; the orderly discharge is a "Prometheus unbound," or a "L'age d'airain," according to the special aptitudes of the enthused person. But it must be remembered that special aptitudes are very easy to acquire if the driving force of enthusiasm be great. If you cannot keep the rules of others, you make rules of your own. One set turns out in the long run to be just as good as another.

Henri Rousseau, the douanier, was laughed at all his life. I laughed as heartily as the rest; though, almost despite myself, I kept on saying (as the phrase goes) "that I felt something; couldn't say what."

The moment it occurred to somebody to put up all his paintings in one room by themselves, it was instantly apparent that his *naïveté* was the simplicity of a Master.

Let no one then imagine that I fail to perceive or underestimate the dangers of employing these methods. The

34

occurrence even of so simple a matter as fatigue might change a Las Meninas into a stupid sexual crisis.

It will be necessary for most Englishmen to emulate the self-control of the Arabs and Hindus, whose ideal is to deflower the greatest possible number of virgins—eighty is considered a fairly good performance—without completing the act.

It is, indeed, of the first importance for the celebrant in any phallic rite to be able to complete the act without even once allowing a sexual or sensual thought to invade his mind. The mind must be as absolutely detached from one's own body as it is from another person's.

XI

Of musical instruments few are suitable. The human voice is the best, and the only one which can be usefully employed in chorus. Anything like an orchestra implies infinite rehearsal, and introduces an atmosphere of artificiality. The organ is a worthy solo instrument, and is an orchestra in itself, while its tone and associations favour the religious idea.

The violin is the most useful of all, for its every mood expresses the hunger for the infinite, and yet it is so mobile that it has a greater emotional range than any of its competitors. Accompaniment must be dispensed with, unless a harpist be available.

The harmonium is a horrible instrument, if only because of its associations; and the piano is like unto it, although, if unseen and played by a Paderewski, it would serve.

The trumpet and the bell are excellent, to startle, at the crises of a ceremony.

35

ENERGIZED ENTHUSIASM   45

Hot, drubbing, passionate, in a different class of ceremony, a class more intense and direct, but on the whole less exalted, the tom-tom stands alone. It combines well with the practice of mantra, and is the best accompaniment for any sacred dance.

XII

Of sacred dances the most practical for a gathering is the seated dance. One sits cross-legged on the floor, and sways to and fro from the hips in time with the mantra. A solo or duet of dancers as a spectacle rather distracts from this exercise. I would suggest a very small and very brilliant light on the floor in the middle of the room. Such a room is best floored with mosaic marble; an ordinary Freemason's Lodge carpet is not a bad thing.

The eyes, if they see anything at all, see then only the rhythmical or mechanical squares leading in perspective to the simple unwinking light.

The swinging of the body with the mantra (which has a habit of rising and falling as if of its own accord in a very weird way) becomes more accentuated; ultimately a curiously spasmodic stage occurs, and then the consciousness flickers and goes out; perhaps breaks through into the divine consciousness, perhaps is merely recalled to itself by some variable in external impression.

The above is a very simple description of a very simple and earnest form of ceremony, based entirely upon rhythm.

It is very easy to prepare, and its results are usually very encouraging for the beginner.

36

ENERGIZED ENTHUSIASM

XIII

Wine being a mocker and strong drink raging, its use is more likely to lead to trouble than mere music.

One essential difficulty is dosage. One needs exactly enough; and, as Blake points out, one can only tell what is enough by taking too much. For each man the dose varies enormously; so does it for the same man at different times.

The ceremonial escape from this is to have a noiseless attendant to bear the bowl of libation, and present it to each in turn, at frequent intervals. Small doses should be drunk, and the bowl passed on, taken as the worshipper deems advisable. Yet the cup-bearer should be an initiate, and use his own discretion before presenting the bowl. The slightest sign that intoxication is mastering the man should be a sign to him to pass that man. This practice can be easily fitted to the ceremony previously described.

If desired, instead of wine, the elixir introduced by me to Europe may be employed. But its results, if used in this way, have not as yet been thoroughly studied. It is my immediate purpose to repair this neglect.

XIV

The sexual excitement, which must complete the harmony of method, offers a more difficult problem.

It is exceptionally desirable that the actual bodily movements involved should be decorous in the highest sense, and many people are so ill-trained that they will be unable to regard such a ceremony with any but critical or lascivious

37

eyes; either would be fatal to all the good already done. It is presumably better to wait until all present are greatly exalted before risking a profanation.

It is not desirable, in my opinion, that the ordinary worshippers should celebrate in public.

The sacrifice should be single.

Whether or no . . .

XV

Thus far had I written when the distinguished poet, whose conversation with me upon the Mysteries had incited me to jot down these few rough notes, knocked at my door. I told him that I was at work on the ideas suggested by him, and that—well, I was rather stuck. He asked permission to glance at the MS. (for he reads English fluently, though speaking but a few words), and having done so, kindled and said: "If you come with me now, we will finish your essay." Glad enough of any excuse to stop working, the more plausible the better, I hastened to take down my coat and hat.

"By the way," he remarked in the automobile, "I take it that you do not mind giving me the Word of Rose Croix." Surprised, I exchanged the secrets of I.N.R.I. with him. "And now, very excellent and perfect Prince," he said, "what follows is under this seal." And he gave me the most solemn of all Masonic tokens. "You are about," said he, "to compare your ideal with our real."

He touched a bell. The automobile stopped, and we got out. He dismissed the chauffeur. "Come," he said, "we have a brisk half-mile." We walked through thick woods to
3⁸

an old house, where we were greeted in silence by a gentleman who, though in court dress, wore a very "practicable" sword. On satisfying him, we were passed through a corridor to an anteroom, where another armed guardian awaited us. He, after a further examination, proceeded to offer me a court dress, the insignia of a Sovereign Prince of Rose Croix, and a garter and mantle, the former of green silk, the latter of green velvet, and lined with cerise silk. "It is a low mass," whispered the guardian. In this anteroom were three or four others, both ladies and gentlemen, busily robing.

In a third room we found a procession formed, and joined it. There were twenty-six of us in all. Passing a final guardian we reached the chapel itself, at whose entrance stood a young man and a young woman, both dressed in simple robes of white silk embroidered with gold, red and blue. The former bore a torch of resinous wood, the latter sprayed us as we passed with attar of roses from a cup.

The room in which we now were had at one time been a chapel; so much its shape declared. But the high altar was covered with a cloth that displayed the Rose and Cross, while above it were ranged seven candelabra, each of seven branches.

The stalls had been retained; and at each knight's hand burned a taper of rose-coloured wax, and a bouquet of roses was before him.

In the centre of the nave was a great cross—a "calvary cross of ten squares," measuring, say, six feet by five—painted in red upon a white board, at whose edge were rings through which passed gilt staves. At each corner was a banner, bearing lion, bull, eagle and man, and from the top of their

39

staves sprang a canopy of blue, wherein were figured in gold the twelve emblems of the Zodiac.

Knights and Dames being installed, suddenly a bell tinkled in the architrave. Instantly all rose. The doors opened at a trumpet peal from without, and a herald advanced, followed by the High Priest and Priestess.

The High Priest was a man of nearly sixty years, if I may judge by the white beard ; but he walked with the springy yet assured step of the thirties. The High Priestess, a proud, tall sombre woman of perhaps thirty summers, walked by his side, their hands raised and touching as in the minuet. Their trains were borne by the two youths who had admitted us.

All this while an unseen organ played an Introit.

This ceased as they took their places at the altar. They faced West, waiting.

On the closing of the doors the armed guard, who was clothed in a scarlet robe instead of green, drew his sword, and went up and down the aisle, chanting exorcisms and swinging the great sword. All present drew their swords and faced outward, holding the points in front of them. This part of the ceremony appeared interminable. When it was over the girl and boy reappeared ; bearing, the one a bowl, the other a censer. Singing some litany or other, apparently in Greek, though I could not catch the words, they purified and consecrated the chapel.

Now the High Priest and High Priestess began a litany in rhythmic lines of equal length. At each third response they touched hands in a peculiar manner ; at each seventh they kissed. The twenty-first was a complete embrace. The bell tinkled in the architrave ; and they parted. The High Priest

40

then took from the altar a flask curiously shaped to imitate a phallus. The High Priestess knelt and presented a boat-shaped cup of gold. He knelt opposite her, and did not pour from the flask.

Now the Knights and Dames began a long litany; first a Dame in treble, then a Knight in bass, then a response in chorus of all present with the organ. This Chorus was:

EVOE HO, IACCHE! EPELTHON, EPELTHON, EVOE, IAO!

Again and again it rose and fell. Towards its close, whether by "stage effect" or no I could not swear, the light over the altar grew rosy, then purple. The High Priest sharply and suddenly threw up his hand; instant silence.

He now poured out the wine from the flask. The High Priestess gave it to the girl attendant, who bore it to all present.

This was no ordinary wine. It has been said of vodki that it looks like water and tastes like fire. With this wine the reverse is the case. It was of a rich fiery gold in which flames of light danced and shook, but its taste was limpid and pure like fresh spring water. No sooner had I drunk of it, however, than I began to tremble. It was a most astonishing sensation; I can imagine a man feel thus as he awaits his executioner, when he has passed through fear, and is all excitement.

I looked down my stall, and saw that each was similarly affected. During the libation the High Priestess sang a hymn, again in Greek. This time I recognized the words; they were those of an ancient Ode to Aphrodite.

The boy attendant now descended to the red cross, stooped and kissed it; then he danced upon it in such a way that he

41

seemed to be tracing the patterns of a marvellous rose of gold, for the percussion caused a shower of bright dust to fall from the canopy. Meanwhile the litany (different words, but the same chorus) began again. This time it was a duet between the High Priest and Priestess. At each chorus Knights and Dames bowed low. The girl moved round continuously, and the bowl passed.

This ended in the exhaustion of the boy, who fell fainting on the cross. The girl immediately took the bowl and put it to his lips. Then she raised him, and, with the assistance of the Guardian of the Sanctuary, led him out of the chapel.

The bell again tinkled in the architrave.

The herald blew a fanfare.

The High Priest and High Priestess moved stately to each other and embraced, in the act unloosing the heavy golden robes which they wore. These fell, twin lakes of gold. I now saw her dressed in a garment of white watered silk, lined throughout (as it appeared later) with ermine.

The High Priest's vestment was an elaborate embroidery of every colour, harmonized by exquisite yet robust art. He wore also a breastplate corresponding to the canopy; a sculptured "beast" at each corner in gold, while the twelve signs of the Zodiac were symbolized by the stones of the breastplate.

The bell tinkled yet again, and the herald again sounded his trumpet. The celebrants moved hand in hand down the nave while the organ thundered forth its solemn harmonies.

All the Knights and Dames rose and gave the secret sign of the Rose Croix.

It was at this part of the ceremony that things began to

42

happen to me. I became suddenly aware that my body had lost both weight and tactile sensibility. My consciousness seemed to be situated no longer in my body. I "mistook myself," if I may use the phrase, for one of the stars in the canopy.

In this way I missed seeing the celebrants actually approach the cross. The bell tinkled again ; I came back to myself, and then I saw that the High Priestess, standing at the foot of the cross, had thrown her robe over it, so that the cross was no longer visible. There was only a board covered with ermine. She was now naked but for her coloured and jewelled head-dress and the heavy torque of gold about her neck, and the armlets and anklets that matched it. She began to sing in a soft strange tongue, so low and smoothly that in my partial bewilderment I could not hear all ; but I caught a few words, Io Paian ! Io Pan ! and a phrase in which the words Iao Sabao ended emphatically a sentence in which I caught the words Eros, Thelema and Sebazo.

While she did this she unloosed the breastplate and gave it to the girl attendant. The robe followed ; I saw that they were naked and unashamed. For the first time there was absolute silence.

Now, from an hundred jets surrounding the board poured forth a perfumed purple smoke. The world was wrapt in a fond gauze of mist, sacred as the clouds upon the mountains.

Then at a signal given by the High Priest, the bell tinkled once more. The celebrants stretched out their arms in the form of a cross, interlacing their fingers. Slowly they revolved through three circles and a half. She then laid him down upon the cross, and took her own appointed place.

43

The organ now again rolled forth its solemn music.

I was lost to everything. Only this I saw, that the celebrants made no expected motion. The movements were extremely small and yet extremely strong.

This must have continued for a great length of time. To me it seemed as if eternity itself could not contain the variety and depth of my experiences. Tongue nor pen could record them ; and yet I am fain to attempt the impossible.

1. I was, certainly and undoubtedly, the star in the canopy. This star was an incomprehensibly enormous world of pure flame.

2. I suddenly realized that the star was of no size whatever. It was not that the star shrank, but that it ($=$ I) became suddenly conscious of infinite space.

3. An explosion took place. I was in consequence a point of light, infinitely small, yet infinitely bright, and this point was *without position*.

4. Consequently this point was ubiquitous, and there was a feeling of infinite bewilderment, blinded after a very long time by a gush of infinite rapture (I use the word " blinded " as if under constraint ; I should have preferred to use the words "blotted out " or "overwhelmed " or " illuminated ").

5. This infinite fullness—I have not described it as such, but it was that—was suddenly changed into a feeling of infinite emptiness, which became conscious as a yearning.

6. These two feelings began to alternate, always with suddenness, and without in any way overlapping, with great rapidity.

7. This alternation must have occurred fifty times—I had rather have said an hundred.

44

ENERGIZED ENTHUSIASM

8. The two feelings suddenly became one. Again the word explosion is the only one that gives any idea of it.

9. I now seemed to be conscious of everything at once, that it was at the same time *one* and *many*. I say "at once," that is, I was not successively all things, but instantaneously.

10. This being, if I may call it being, seemed to drop into an infinite abyss of Nothing.

11. While this "falling" lasted, the bell suddenly tinkled three times. I instantly became my normal self, yet with a constant awareness, which has never left me to this hour, that the truth of the matter is not this normal "I" but "That" which is still dropping into Nothing. I am assured by those who know that I may be able to take up the thread if I attend another ceremony.

The tinkle died away. The girl attendant ran quickly forward and folded the ermine over the celebrants. The herald blew a fanfare, and the Knights and Dames left their stalls. Advancing to the board, we took hold of the gilded carrying poles, and followed the herald in procession out of the chapel, bearing the litter to a small side-chapel leading out of the middle anteroom, where we left it, the guard closing the doors.

In silence we disrobed, and left the house. About a mile through the woods we found my friend's automobile waiting.

I asked him, if that was a low mass, might I not be permitted to witness a High Mass?

"Perhaps," he answered with a curious smile, "if all they tell of you is true."

In the meanwhile he permitted me to describe the ceremony and its results as faithfully as I was able, charging me only to give no indication of the city near which it took place.

45

I am willing to indicate to initiates of the Rose Croix degree of Masonry under proper charter from the genuine authorities (for there are spurious Masons working under a forged charter) the address of a person willing to consider their fitness to affiliate to a Chapter practising similar rites.

XVI

I consider it supererogatory to continue my essay on the Mysteries and my analysis of *Energized Enthusiasm*.

46

LIBER

XXXVI

THE

STAR

SAPPHIRE

THE STAR SAPPHIRE

Let the Adept be armed with his Magick Rood (and provided with his mystic Rose).

In the centre, let him give the L.V.X. signs; or if he know them, if he will and dare do them, and can keep silent about them, the signs of N.O.X. being the signs of Puer, Vir, Puella, Mulier. Omit the sign I.R.

Then let him advance to the East and make the Holy Hexagram, saying: *Pater et Mater unus deus Ararita.*

Let him go round to the South, make the Holy Hexagram and say: *Mater et Filius unus deus Ararita.*

Let him go round to the West, make the Holy Hexagram and say: *Filius et Filia unus deus Ararita.*

Let him go round to the North, make the Holy Hexagram and then say: *Filia et Pater unus deus Ararita.*

Let him then return to the Centre, and so to The Centre of All (making the *Rosy Cross* as he may know how) saying *Ararita Ararita Ararita.*

(In this the Signs shall be those of Set Triumphant and of Baphomet. Also shall Set appear in the Circle. Let him drink of the Sacrament and let him communicate the same.) Then let him say: *Omnia in Duos: Duo in Unum:*

321

Unus in Nihil: Haec nec Quatuor nec Omnia nec Duo nec Unus nec Nihil Sunt.

Gloria Patri et Matri et Filio et Filiae et Spiritui Sancto externo et Spiritui Sancto interno ut erat est erit in saecula Saeculorum sex in uno per nomen Septem in uno Ararita.

Let him then repeat the signs of L.V.X. but not the signs of N.O.X.: for it is not he that shall arise in the Sign of Isis Rejoicing.

LIBER A'ASH

VEL

CAPRICORNI PNEVMATICI

SVB FIGVRÂ

CCCLXX

A∴A∴
Publication in Class A.
Imprimatur:
N. Fra A∴A∴

LIBER A'ASH

VEL CAPRICORNI PNEVMATICI

SVB FIGVRÂ CCCLXX

0. Gnarled Oak of God ! In thy branches is the lightning nested ! Above thee hangs the Eyeless Hawk.

1. Thou art blasted and black ! Supremely solitary in that heath of scrub.

2. Up ! The ruddy clouds hang over thee ! It is the storm.

3. There is a flaming gash in the sky.

4. Up.

5. Thou art tossed about in the grip of the storm for an æon and an æon and an æon. But thou givest not thy sap ; thou fallest not.

6. Only in the end shalt thou give up thy sap when the great God F. I. A. T. is enthroned on the day of Be-with-Us.

7. For two things are done and a third thing is begun. Isis and Osiris are given over to incest and adultery. Horus leaps up thrice armed from the womb of his mother. Harpocrates his twin is hidden within him. Set is his holy covenant, that he shall display in the great day of M. A. A. T., that is being interpreted the Master of the Temple of A∴, A∴, whose name is Truth.

35

8. Now in this is the magical power known.

9. It is like the oak that hardens itself and bears up against the storm. It is weather-beaten and scarred and confident like a sea-captain.

10. Also it straineth like a hound in the leash.

11. It hath pride and great subtlety. Yea, and glee also!

12. Let the magus act thus in his conjuration.

13. Let him sit and conjure ; let him draw himself together in that forcefulness ; let him rise next swollen and straining ; let him dash back the hood from his head and fix his basilisk eye upon the sigil of the demon. Then let him sway the force of him to and fro like a satyr in silence, until the Word burst from his throat.

14. Then let him not fall exhausted, although the might have been ten thousandfold the human ; but that which floodeth him is the infinite mercy of the Genitor-Genetrix of the Universe, whereof he is the Vessel.

15. Nor do thou deceive thyself. It is easy to tell the live force from the dead matter. It is no easier to tell the live snake from the dead snake.

16. Also concerning vows. Be obstinate, and be not obstinate. Understand that the yielding of the Yoni is one with the lengthening of the Lingam. Thou art both these ; and thy vow is but the rustling of the wind on Mount Meru.

17. Now shalt thou adore me who am the Eye and the Tooth, the Goat of the Spirit, the Lord of Creation. I am the Eye in the Triangle, the Silver Star that ye adore.

18. I am Baphomet, that is the Eightfold Word that shall be equilibrated with the Three.

36

19. There is no act or passion that shall not be a hymn in mine honour.

20. All holy things and all symbolic things shall be my sacraments.

21. These animals are sacred unto me; the goat, and the duck, and the ass, and the gazelle, the man, the woman and the child.

22. All corpses are sacred unto me; they shall not be touched save in mine eucharist. All lonely places are sacred unto me; where one man gathereth himself together in my name, there will I leap forth in the midst of him.

23. I am the hideous god; and who mastereth me is uglier than I.

24. Yet I give more than Bacchus and Apollo; my gifts exceed the olive and the horse.

25. Who worshippeth me must worship me with many rites.

26. I am concealed with all concealments; when the Most Holy Ancient One is stripped and driven through the market-place I am still secret and apart.

27. Whom I love I chastise with many rods.

28. All things are sacred to me; no thing is sacred from me.

29. For there is no holiness where I am not.

30. Fear not when I fall in the fury of the storm; for mine acorns are blown afar by the wind; and verily I shall rise again, and my children about me, so that we shall uplift our forest in Eternity.

31. Eternity is the storm that covereth me.

32. I am Existence, the Existence that existeth not save through its own Existence, that is beyond the Existence of

37

Existences, and rooted deeper than the No-Thing-Tree in the Land of No-Thing.

33. Now therefore thou knowest when I am within thee, when my hood is spread over thy skull, when my might is more than the penned Indus, and resistless as the Giant Glacier.

34. For as thou art before a lewd woman in Thy nakedness in the bazar, sucked up by her slyness and smiles, so art thou wholly and no more in part before the symbol of the beloved, though it be but a Pisacha or a Yantra or a Deva.

35. And in all shalt thou create the Infinite Bliss, and the next link of the Infinite Chain.

36. This chain reaches from Eternity to Eternity, ever in triangles—is not my symbol a triangle?—ever in circles—is not the symbol of the Beloved a circle? Therein is all progress base illusion, for every circle is alike and every triangle alike!

37. But the progress is progress, and progress is rapture, constant, dazzling, showers of light, waves of dew, flames of the hair of the Great Goddess, flowers of the roses that are about her neck, Amen!

38. Therefore lift up thyself as I am lifted up. Hold thyself in as I am master to accomplish. At the end, be the end far distant as the stars that lie in the navel of Nuit, do thou slay thyself as I at the end am slain, in the death that is life, in the peace that is mother of war, in the darkness that holds light in his hand as a harlot that plucks a jewel from her nostrils.

39. So therefore the beginning is delight, and the End is delight, and delight is in the midst, even as the Indus is

38

LIBER A'ASH

water in the cavern of the glacier, and water among the greater hills and the lesser hills and through the ramparts of the hills and through the plains, and water at the mouth thereof when it leaps forth into the mighty sea, yea, into the mighty sea.

[The Interpretation of this Book will be given to members of the Grade of Dominus Liminis on application, each to his Adeptus.]

39

LIBER CHETH

VEL

VALLVM ABIEGNI

SVB FIGVRÂ

CLVI

A∴A∴
Publication in Class A.
Imprimatur:
N. Fra A∴A∴

LIBER CHETH

VEL VALLUM ABIEGNI

SVB FIGVRÂ CLVI

1. This is the secret of the Holy Graal, that is the sacred vessel of our Lady the Scarlet Woman, Babalon the Mother of Abominations, the bride of Chaos, that rideth upon our Lord the Beast.

2. Thou shalt drain out thy blood that is thy life into the golden cup of her fornication.

3. Thou shalt mingle thy life with the universal life. Thou shalt keep not back one drop.

4. Then shall thy brain be dumb, and thy heart beat no more, and all thy life shall go from thee; and thou shalt be cast out upon the midden, and the birds of the air shall feast upon thy flesh, and thy bones shall whiten in the sun.

5. Then shall the winds gather themselves together, and bear thee up as it were a little heap of dust in a sheet that hath four corners, and they shall give it unto the guardians of the abyss.

6. And because there is no life therein, the guardians of the abyss shall bid the angels of the winds pass by. And the angels shall lay thy dust in the City of the Pyramids, and the name thereof shall be no more.

25

7. Now therefore that thou mayest achieve this ritual of the Holy Graal, do thou divest thyself of all thy goods.

8. Thou hast wealth; give it unto them that have need thereof, yet no desire toward it.

9. Thou hast health; slay thyself in the fervour of thine abandonment unto Our Lady. Let thy flesh hang loose upon thy bones, and thine eyes glare with thy quenchless lust unto the Infinite, with thy passion for the Unknown, for Her that is beyond Knowledge the accursèd one.

10. Thou hast love; tear thy mother from thine heart, and spit in the face of thy father. Let thy foot trample the belly of thy wife, and let the babe at her breast be the prey of dogs and vultures.

11. For if thou dost not this with thy will, then shall We do this despite thy will. So that thou attain to the Sacrament of the Graal in the Chapel of Abominations.

12. And behold! if by stealth thou keep unto thyself one thought of thine, then shalt thou be cast out into the abyss for ever; and thou shalt be the lonely one, the eater of dung, the afflicted in the Day of Be-with-Us.

13. Yea! verily this is the Truth, this is the Truth, this is the Truth. Unto thee shall be granted joy and health and wealth and wisdom when thou art no longer thou.

14. Then shall every gain be a new sacrament, and it shall not defile thee; thou shalt revel with the wanton in the market-place, and the virgins shall fling roses upon thee, and the merchants bend their knees and bring thee gold and spices. Also young boys shall pour wonderful wines for thee, and the singers and the dancers shall sing and dance for thee.

26

15. Yet shalt thou not be therein, for thou shalt be forgotten, dust lost in dust.

16. Nor shall the æon itself avail thee in this; for from the dust shall a white ash be prepared by Hermes the Invisible.

17. And this is the wrath of God, that these things should be thus.

18. And this is the grace of God, that these things should be thus.

19. Wherefore I charge you that ye come unto me in the Beginning; for if ye take but one step in this Path, ye must arrive inevitably at the end thereof.

20. This Path is beyond Life and Death; it is also beyond Love; but that ye know not, for ye know not Love.

21. And the end thereof is known not even unto Our Lady or to the Beast whereon She rideth; nor unto the Virgin her daughter nor unto Chaos her lawful Lord; but unto the Crowned Child is it known? It is not known if it be known.

22. Therefore unto Hadit and unto Nuit be the glory in the End and the Beginning; yea, in the End and the Beginning.

27

LIBER STELLÆ RUBEÆ

A secret ritual of Apep, the Heart of IAO-OAI, delivered unto V.V.V.V.V. for his use in a certain matter of Liber Legis, and written down under the figure

LXVI

A ∴ A ∴
Publication in Class A.
Imprimatur :
N. Fra A ∴ A ∴

LIBER STELLÆ RUBEÆ

1. Apep deifieth Asar.

2. Let excellent virgins evoke rejoicing, son of Night !

3. This is the book of the most secret cult of the Ruby Star. It shall be given to none, save to the shameless in deed as in word.

4. No man shall understand this writing—it is too subtle for the sons of men.

5. If the Ruby Star have shed its blood upon thee ; if in the season of the moon thou hast invoked by the Iod and the Pe, then mayst thou partake of this most secret sacrament.

6. One shall instruct another, with no care for the matters of men's thought.

7. There shall be a fair altar in the midst, extended upon a black stone.

8. At the head of the altar gold, and twin images in green of the Master.

9. In the midst a cup of green wine.

10. At the foot the Star of Ruby.

11. The altar shall be entirely bare.

12. First, the ritual of the Flaming Star.

13. Next, the ritual of the Seal.

31

14. Next, the infernal adorations of Oai.

> Mu pa telai,
> Tu wa melai
> ā, ā, ā.
> Tu fu tulu!
> Tu fu tulu
> Pa, Sa, Ga.

> Qwi Mu telai
> Ya Pu melai;
> ū, ū, ū.
> 'Se gu malai;
> Pe fu telai,
> Fu tu lu.

> O chi balae
> Wa pa malae :—
> Ūt! Ūt! Ūt!
> Ge; fu latrai,
> Le fu malai
> Kūt! Hūt! Nūt!

> Al Ōāī
> Rel moai
> Ti—Ti—Ti!
> Wa la pelai
> Tu fu latai
> Wi, Ni, Bi.

15. Also thou shalt excite the wheels with the five wounds and the five wounds.

16. Then thou shalt excite the wheels with the two and

32

the third in the midst; even ♄ and ♃, ☉ and ♋, ♂ and ♀, and ☿.

17. Then the five—and the sixth.

18. Also the altar shall fume before the master with incense that hath no smoke.

19. That which is to be denied shall be denied; that which is to be trampled shall be trampled; that which is to be spat upon shall be spat upon.

20. These things shall be burnt in the outer fire.

21. Then again the master shall speak as he will soft words, and with music and what else he will bring forward the Victim.

22. Also he shall slay a young child upon the altar, and the blood shall cover the altar with perfume as of roses.

23. Then shall the master appear as He should appear—in His glory.

24. He shall stretch himself upon the altar, and awake it into life, and into death.

25. (For so we conceal that life which is beyond.)

26. The temple shall be darkened, save for the fire and the lamp of the altar.

27. There shall he kindle a great fire and a devouring.

28. Also he shall smite the altar with his scourge, and blood shall flow therefrom.

29. Also he shall have made roses bloom thereon.

30. In the end he shall offer up the Vast Sacrifice, at the moment when the God licks up the flame upon the altar.

31. All these things shalt thou perform strictly, observing the time.

32. And the Beloved shall abide with Thee.

33

33. Thou shalt not disclose the interior world of this rite unto any one : therefore have I written it in symbols that cannot be understood.

34. I who reveal the ritual am Iao and Oai ; the Right and the Averse.

35. These are alike unto me.

36. Now the Veil of this operation is called Shame, and the Glory abideth within.

37. Thou shalt comfort the heart of the secret stone with the warm blood. Thou shalt make a subtle decoction of delight, and the Watchers shall drink thereof.

38. I, Apep the Serpent, am the heart of Iao. Isis shall await Asar, and I in the midst.

39. Also the Priestess shall seek another altar, and perform my ceremonies thereon.

40. There shall be no hymn nor dithyramb in my praise and the praise of the rite, seeing that it is utterly beyond.

41. Thou shalt assure thyself of the stability of the altar.

42. In this rite thou shalt be alone.

43. I will give thee another ceremony whereby many shall rejoice.

44. Before all let the Oath be taken firmly as thou raisest up the altar from the black earth.

45. In the words that Thou knowest.

46. For I also swear unto thee by my body and soul that shall never be parted in sunder that I dwell within thee coiled and ready to spring.

47. I will give thee the kingdoms of the earth, O thou Who hast mastered the kingdoms of the East and of the West.

34

LIBER STELLÆ RUBEÆ

48. I am Apep, O thou slain One. Thou shalt slay thyself upon mine altar : I will have thy blood to drink.

49. For I am a mighty vampire, and my children shall suck up the wine of the earth which is blood.

50. Thou shalt replenish thy veins from the chalice of heaven.

51. Thou shalt be secret, a fear to the world.

52. Thou shalt be exalted, and none shall see thee ; exalted, and none shall suspect thee.

53. For there are two glories diverse, and thou who hast won the first shalt enjoy the second.

54. I leap with joy within thee ; my head is arisen to strike.

55. O the lust, the sheer rapture, of the life of the snake in the spine !

56. Mightier than God or man, I am in them, and pervade them.

57. Follow out these my words.

58. Fear nothing.
Fear nothing.
Fear nothing.

59. For I am nothing, and me thou shalt fear, O my virgin, my prophet within whose bowels I rejoice.

60. Thou shalt fear with the fear of love: I will overcome thee.

61. Thou shalt be very nigh to death.

62. But I will overcome thee ; the New Life shall illumine thee with the Light that is beyond the Stars.

63. Thinkest thou ? I, the force that have created all, am not to be despised.

64. And I will slay thee in my lust.

35

65. Thou shalt scream with the joy and the pain and the fear and the love—so that the ΛΟΓΟΣ of a new God leaps out among the Stars.

66. There shall be no sound heard but this thy lion-roar of rapture ; yea, this thy lion-roar of rapture.

36

ASTARTÉ

VEL

LIBER BERYLLI
SVB FIGVRÅ
CLXXV

A∴A∴.
Publication in Class B.
Imprimatur:
N. Fra A∴A∴.

LIBER ASTARTÉ

VEL BERYLLI

SVB FIGVRÂ CLXXV

o. This is the book of Uniting Himself to a particular Deity by devotion.

1. *Considerations before the Threshold.* First, concerning the choice of a particular Deity. This matter is of no import, sobeit that thou choose one suited to thine own highest nature. Howsoever, this method is not so suitable for gods austere as Saturn, or intellectual as Thoth. But for such deities as in themselves partake in anywise of love it is a perfect mode.

2. *Concerning the prime method of this Magick Art.* Let the devotee consider well that although Christ and Osiris be one, yet the former is to be worshipped with Christian, and the latter with Egyptian rites. And this although the rites themselves are ceremonially equivalent. There should, however, be *one* symbol declaring the transcending of such limitations; and with regard to the Deity also, there should be some *one* affirmation of his identity both with all other similar gods of other nations, and with the Supreme of whom all are but partial reflections.

3. *Concerning the chief place of devotion.* This is the Heart of the devotee, and should be symbolically represented

39

by that room or spot which he loves best. And the dearest spot therein shall be the shrine of his temple. It is most convenient if this shrine and altar should be sequestered in woods, or in a private grove, or garden. But let it be protected from the profane.

4. *Concerning the Image of the Deity.* Let there be an image of the Deity; first, because in meditation there is mindfulness induced thereby; and second, because a certain power enters and inhabits it by virtue of the ceremonies; or so it is said, and We deny it not. Let this image be the most beautiful and perfect which the devotee is able to procure; or if he be able to paint or to carve the same, it is all the better. As for Deities with whose nature no Image is compatible, let them be worshipped in an empty shrine. Such are Brahma and Allah. Also some post-captivity conceptions of Jehovah.

5. *Further concerning the shrine.* Let this shrine be furnished appropriately as to its ornaments, according to the book 777. With ivy and pine-cones, that is to say, for Bacchus, and let lay before him both grapes and wine. So also for Ceres let there be corn, and cakes; or for Diana moon-wort and pale herbs, and pure water. Further, it is well to support the shrine with talismans of the planets, signs and elements appropriate. But these should be made according to the right Ingenium of the Philosophus by the light of the Book 777 during the course of his Devotion. It is also well, nevertheless, if a magick circle with the right signs and names be made beforehand.

6. *Concerning the ceremonies.* Let the Philosophus prepare a powerful Invocation of the particular Deity, according to his Ingenium. But let it consist of these several parts:

40

LIBER ASTARTÉ

First, an Imprecation, as of a slave unto his Lord.

Second, an Oath, as of a vassal to his Liege.

Third, a Memorial, as of a child to his Parent.

Fourth, an Orison, as of a Priest unto his God.

Fifth, a Colloquy, as of a Brother with his Brother.

Sixth, a Conjuration, as of a Friend with his Friend.

Seventh, a Madrigal, as of a Lover to his Mistress.

And mark well that the first should be of awe, the second of fealty, the third of dependence, the fourth of adoration, the fifth of confidence, the sixth of comradeship, the seventh of passion.

7. *Further concerning the ceremonies.* Let then this Invocation be the principal part of an ordered ceremony. And in this ceremony let the Philosophus in no wise neglect the service of a menial. Let him sweep and garnish the place, sprinkling it with water or with wine as is appropriate to the particular Deity, and consecrating it with oil, and with such ritual as may seem him best. And let all be done with intensity and minuteness.

8. *Concerning the period of devotion, and the hours thereof.* Let a fixed period be set for the worship; and it is said that the least time is nine days by seven, and the greatest seven years by nine. And concerning the hours, let the Ceremony be performed every day thrice, or at least once, and let the sleep of the Philosophus be broken for some purpose of devotion at least once in every night.

Now to some it may seem best to appoint fixed hours for the ceremony, to others it may seem that the ceremony should be performed as the spirit moves them so to do : for this there is no rule.

41

9. *Concerning the Robes and Instruments.* The Wand and Cup are to be chosen for this Art; never the Sword or Dagger, never the Pantacle, unless that Pantacle chance to be of a nature harmonious. But even so it is best to keep the Wand and Cup; and if one must choose, the Cup.

For the Robes, that of a Philosophus, or that of an Adept Within is most suitable; or, the robe best fitted for the service of the particular Deity, as a bassara for Bacchus, a white robe for Vesta. So also, for Vesta, one might use for instrument the Lamp; or the sickle, for Chronos.

10. *Concerning the Incense and Libations.* The incense should follow the nature of the particular Deity; as, mastic for Mercury, dittany for Persephone. Also the libations, as, a decoction of nightshade for Melancholia, or of Indian hemp for Uranus.

11. *Concerning the harmony of the ceremonies.* Let all these things be rightly considered, and at length, in language of the utmost beauty at the command of the Philosophus, accompanied, if he have skill, by music, and interwoven, if the particular Deity be jocund, with dancing. And all being carefully prepared and rehearsed, let it be practised daily until it be wholly rhythmical with his aspiration, and as it were, a part of his being.

12. *Concerning the variety of the ceremonies.* Now, seeing that every man differeth essentially from every other man, albeit in essence he is identical, let also these ceremonies assert their identity by their diversity. For this reason do We leave much herein to the right Ingenium of the Philosophus.

13. *Concerning the life of the devotee.* First, let his way of life be such as is pleasing to the particular Deity. Thus to

42

invoke Neptune, let him go a-fishing; but if Hades, let him not approach the water that is hateful to Him.

14. *Further, concerning the life of the devotee.* Let him cut away from his life any act, word, or thought, that is hateful to the particular Deity; as, unchastity in the case of Artemis, evasions in the case of Ares. Besides this, he should avoid all harshness or unkindness of any kind in thought, word, or deed, seeing that above the particular Deity is One in whom all is One. Yet also he may deliberately practise cruelties, where the particular Deity manifests His love in that manner; as in the case of Kali, and of Pan. And therefore, before the beginning of his period of devotion, let him practise according to the rules of Liber Jugorum.

15. *Further concerning the life of the devotee.* Now, as many are fully occupied with their affairs, let it be known that this method is adaptable to the necessities of all.

And We bear witness that this which followeth is the Crux and Quintessence of the whole Method.

First, if he have no Image, let him take anything soever, and consecrate it as an Image of his God. Likewise with his robes and instruments, his suffumigations and libations: for his Robe hath he not a night-dress; for his instrument a walking-stick; for his suffumigation a burning match, for his libation a glass of water?

But let him consecrate each thing that he useth to the service of that particular Deity, and not profane the same to any other use.

16. *Continuation.* Next, concerning his time, if it be short. Let him labour mentally upon his Invocation, concentrating it, and let him perform this Invocation in his heart whenever

43

he hath the leisure. And let him seize eagerly upon every opportunity for this.

17. *Continuation.* Third, even if he have leisure and preparation, let him seek ever to bring inward the symbols, so that even in his well-ordered shrine the whole ceremony revolve inwardly in his heart, that is to say in the temple of his body, of which the outer temple is but an image.

For in the brain is the shrine, and there is no Image therein ; and the breath of man is the incense and the libation.

18. *Continuation.* Further concerning occupation. Let the devotee transmute within the alembic of his heart every thought, or word, or act into the spiritual gold of his devotion.

As thus: eating. Let him say: " I eat this food in gratitude to my Deity that hath sent it to me, in order to gain strength for my devotion to Him."

Or: sleeping. Let him say: " I lie down to sleep, giving thanks for this blessing from my Deity, in order that I may be refreshed for new devotion to Him."

Or: reading. Let him say: " I read this book that I may study the nature of my Deity, that further knowledge of Him may inspire me with deeper devotion to Him."

Or: working. Let him say: " I drive my spade into the earth that fresh flowers (fruit, or what not) may spring up to His glory, and that I, purified by toil, may give better devotion to Him."

Or, whatever it may be that he is doing, let him reason it out in his own mind, drawing it through circumstance and circumstance to that one end and conclusion of the matter. And let him not perform the act until he hath done this.

44

LIBER ASTARTÉ

As it is written : Liber VII. cap. v.—

22. " Every breath, every word, every thought, is an act of love with thee.

23. " The beat of my heart is the pendulum of love.

24. " The songs of me are the soft sighs :

25. " The thoughts of me are very rapture :

26. " And my deeds are the myriads of Thy children, the stars and the atoms."

And Remember Well, that if thou wert in truth a lover, all this wouldst thou do of thine own nature without the slightest flaw or failure in the minutest part thereof.

19. *Concerning the Lections.* Let the Philosophus read solely in his copies of the holy books of Thelema, during the whole period of his devotion. But if he weary, then let him read books which have no part whatever in love, as for recreation.

But let him copy out each verse of Thelema which bears upon this matter, and ponder them, and comment thereupon. For therein is a wisdom and a magic too deep to utter in any other wise.

20. *Concerning the Meditations.* Herein is the most potent method of attaining unto the End, for him who is thoroughly prepared, being purified by the practice of the Transmutation of deed into devotion, and consecrated by the right performance of the holy ceremonies. Yet herein is danger, for that the Mind is fluid as quicksilver, and bordereth upon the Abyss, and is beset by many sirens and devils that seduce and attack it to destroy it. Therefore let the devotee beware, and precise accurately his meditations, even as a man should build a canal from sea to sea.

21. *Continuation.* Let then the Philosophus meditate

45

upon all love that hath ever stirred him. There is the love of David and of Jonathan, and the love of Abraham and Isaac, and the love of Lear and Cordelia, and the love of Damon and Pythias, and the love of Sappho and Atthis, and the love of Romeo and Juliet, and the love of Dante and Beatrice, and the love of Paolo and Francesca, and the love of Cæsar and Lucrezia Borgia, and the love of Aucassin and Nicolette, and the love of Daphnis and Chloe, and the love of Cornelia and Caius Gracchus, and the love of Bacchus and Ariadne, and the love of Cupid and Psyche, and the love of Endymion and Artemis, and the love of Demeter and Persephone, and the love of Venus and Adonis, and the love of Lakshmi and Vishnu, and the love of Siva and Bhavani, and the love of Buddha and Ananda, and the love of Jesus and John, and many more.

Also there is the love of many saints for their particular deity, as of St Francis of Assisi for Christ, of Sri Sabhapaty Swami for Maheswara, of Abdullah Haji Shirazi for Allah, of St Ignatius Loyola for Mary, and many more.

Now do thou take one such story every night, and enact it in thy mind, grasping each identity with infinite care and zest, and do thou figure thyself as one of the lovers and thy Deity as the other. Thus do thou pass through all adventures of love, not omitting one; and to each do thou conclude: How pale a reflection is this of my love for this Deity!

Yet from each shalt thou draw some knowledge of love, some intimacy with love, that shall aid thee to perfect thy love. Thus learn the humility of love from one, its obedience from another, its intensity from a third, its purity from a fourth, its peace from yet a fifth.

46

LIBER ASTARTÉ

So then thy love being made perfect, it shall be worthy of that perfect love of His.

22. *Further concerning meditation.* Moreover, let the Philosophus imagine to himself that he hath indeed succeeded in his devotion, and that his Lord hath appeared to him, and that they converse as may be fitting.

23. *Concerning the Mysterious Triangle.* Now then as three cords separately may be broken by a child, while those same cords duly twisted may bind a giant, let the Philosophus learn to entwine these three methods of Magic into a Spell.

To this end let him understand that as they are One, because the end is one, so are they One because the method is One, even the method of turning the mind toward the particular Deity by love in every act.

And lest thy twine slip, here is a little cord that wrappeth tightly round and round all, even the Mantram or Continuous Prayer.

24. *Concerning the Mantram or Continuous Prayer.* Let the Philosophus weave the Name of the Particular Deity into a sentence short and rhythmical; as, for Artemis: ἐπελθον, ἐπελθον, Ἀρτεμις; or, for Shiva: Namo Shivaya namaha Aum; or, for Mary: Ave Maria; or, for Pan, χαιρε Σωτηρ κοσμου Ἰω Παν Ἰω Παν; or, for Allah: Hua Allahu alazi lailaha illa Hua.

Let him repeat this day and night without cessation mechanically in his brain, which is thus made ready for the Advent of that Lord, and armed against all other.

25. *Concerning the Active and the Passive.* Let the Philosophus change from the active love of his particular Deity to a state of passive awaiting, even almost a repulsion, the repulsion not of distaste, but of a sublime modesty.

47

LIBER ASTARTÉ　　　　　93

As it is written, Liber LXV. ii. 59. I have called unto Thee,
and I have journeyed unto Thee, and it availed me not. 60. I
waited patiently, and Thou wast with me from the beginning.

Then let him change back to the Active, until a veritable
rhythm is established between the states, as it were the
swinging of a Pendulum. But let him reflect that a vast
intelligence is required for this ; for he must stand as it were
almost without himself to watch those phases of himself.
And to do this is a high Art, and pertaineth not altogether to
the grade of Philosophus. Neither is it of itself helpful, but
rather the reverse, in this especial practice.

26. *Concerning Silence.* Now there may come a time in
the course of this practice when the outward symbols of
devotion cease, when the soul is as it were dumb in the
presence of its God. Mark that this is not a cessation, but a
transmutation of the barren seed of prayer into the green
shoot of yearning. This yearning is spontaneous, and it shall
be left to grow, whether it be sweet or bitter. For often
times it is as the torment of hell in which the soul burns and
writhes unceasingly. Yet it ends, and at its end continue
openly thy Method.

27. *Concerning Dryness.* Another state wherein at times
the soul may fall is this dark night. And this is indeed
purifying in such depths that the soul cannot fathom it. It is
less like pain than like death. But it is the necessary death
that comes before the rising of a body glorified.

This state must be endured with fortitude ; and no means
of alleviating it may be employed. It may be broken up by
the breaking up of the whole Method, and a return to the
world without. This cowardice not only destroys the value
48

of all that has gone before, but destroys the value of the Oath of Fealty that thou hast sworn, and makes thy Will a mockery to men and gods.

28. *Concerning the Deceptions of the Devil.* Note well that in this state of dryness a thousand seductions will lure thee away; also a thousand means of breaking thine oath in spirit without breaking it in letter. Against this thou mayst repeat the words of thine oath aloud again and again until the temptation be overcome.

Also the devil will represent to thee that it were much better for this operation that thou do thus and thus, and seek to affright thee by fears for thy health or thy reason.

Or he may send against thee visions worse than madness.

Against all this there is but one remedy, the Discipline of thine Oath. So then thou shalt go through ceremonies meaningless and hideous to thee, and blaspheme shalt thou against thy Deity and curse Him. And this mattereth little, for it is not thou, so be that thou adhere to the Letter of thine Obligation. For thy Spiritual Sight is closed, and to trust it is to be led unto the precipice, and hurled therefrom.

29. *Further of this matter.* Now also subtler than all these terrors are the Illusions of Success. For one instant's self-satisfaction or Expansion of thy Spirit, especially in this state of dryness, and thou art lost. For thou mayst attain the False Union with the Demon himself. Beware also of even the pride which rises from having resisted the temptations.

But so many and so subtle are the wiles of Choronzon that the whole world could not contain their enumeration.

The answer to one and all is the persistence in the literal fulfilment of the routine. Beware, then, last, of that devil

49

who shall whisper in thine ear that the letter killeth, but the spirit giveth life, and answer : Except a corn of wheat fall into the ground and die, it abideth alone ; but if it die, it bringeth forth much fruit.

Yet shalt thou also beware of disputation with the devil, and pride in the cleverness of thine answers to him. Therefore, if thou hast not lost the power of silence, let it be first and last employed against him.

30. *Concerning the Enflaming of the Heart.* Now learn that thy methods are dry one and all. Intellectual exercises, moral exercises, they are not Love. Yet as a man, rubbing two dry sticks together for long, suddenly found a spark, so also from time to time will true love leap unasked into thy meditation. Yet this shall die and be reborn again and again. It may be that thou hast no tinder near.

In the end shall come suddenly a great flame and a devouring, and burn thee utterly.

Now of these sparks, and of these splutterings of flame, and of these beginnings of the Infinite Fire, thou shalt thus be aware. For the sparks thy heart shall leap up, and thy ceremony or meditation or toil shall seem of a sudden to go of its own will ; and for the little flames this shall be increased in volume and intensity ; and for the beginnings of the Infinite Fire thy ceremony shall be caught up unto ravishing song, and thy meditation shall be ecstasy, and thy toil shall be a delight exceeding all pleasure thou hast ever known.

And of the Great Flame that answereth thee it may not be spoken ; for therein is the End of this Magick Art of Devotion.

31. *Considerations with regard to the use of symbols.* It

50

is to be noted that persons of powerful imagination, will, and intelligence have no need of these material symbols. There have been certain saints who are capable of love for an idea as such without it being otherwise than degraded by *idolising* it, to use this word in its true sense. Thus one may be impassioned of beauty, without even the need of so small a concretion of it as "the beauty of Apollo," "the beauty of roses," "the beauty of Attis." Such persons are rare; it may be doubted whether Plato himself attained to any vision of absolute beauty without attaching to it material objects in the first place. A second class is able to contemplate ideals through this veil; a third class need a double veil, and cannot think of the beauty of a rose without a rose before them. For such is this Method of most use; yet let them know that there is this danger therein, that they may mistake the gross body of the symbol for the idea made concrete thereby.

32. *Considerations of further danger to those not purged of material thought.* Let it be remembered that in the nature of the love itself is danger. The lust of the satyr for the nymph is indeed of the same nature as the affinity of Quicklime for water on the one hand, and of the love of Ab for Ama on the other; so also is the triad Osiris, Isis, Horus like that of a horse, mare, foal, and of red, blue, purple. And this is the foundation of Correspondences.

But it were false to say "Horus is a foal" or "Horus is purple." One may say "Horus resembles a foal in this respect, that he is the offspring of two complementary beings."

33. *Further of this matter.* So also many have said truly that all is one, and falsely that since earth is That One, and

51

quality3

ocean is That One, therefore earth is ocean. Unto Him good is illusion, and evil is illusion ; therefore good is evil. By this fallacy of logic are many men destroyed.

Moreover, there are those who take the image for the God ; as who should say, my heart is in Tiphereth, and an Adeptus is in Tiphereth ; I am therefore an adept.

And in this practice the worst danger is this, that the love which is its weapon should fail in one of two ways.

First, if the love lack any quality of love, so long is it not ideal love. For it is written of the Perfected One : " There is no member of my body which is not the member of some god." Therefore let not the Philosophus despise any form of love, but harmonise all. As it is written : Liber LXI. 32. " So therefore Perfection abideth not in the Pinnacles or in the Foundation, but in the harmony of One with all."

Second, if any part of this love exceed, there is disease therein. As, in the love of Othello for Desdemona, love's jealousy overcame love's tenderness, so may it be in this love of a particular Deity. And this is more likely, since in this divine love no element may be omitted.

It is by virtue of this completeness that no human love may in any way attain to more than to forthshadow a little part thereof.

34. *Concerning Mortifications.* These are not necessary to this method. On the contrary, they may destroy the concentration, as counter-irritants to, and so alleviations of, the supreme mortification which is the Absence of the Deity invoked.

Yet as in mortal love arises a distaste for food, or a pleasure in things naturally painful, this perversion should be endured
52

and allowed to take its course. Yet not to the interference with natural bodily health, whereby the instrument of the soul might be impaired.

And concerning sacrifices for love's sake, they are natural to this Method, and right.

But concerning voluntary privations and tortures, without use save as against the devotee, they are generally not natural to healthy natures, and wrong. For they are selfish. To scourge one's self serves not one's master; yet to deny one's self bread that one's child may have cake is the act of a true mother.

35. *Further concerning Mortifications.* If thy body, on which thou ridest, be so disobedient a beast that by no means will he travel in the desired direction, or if thy mind be baulkish and eloquent as Balaam's fabled Ass, then let the practice be abandoned. Let the shrine be covered in sackcloth, and do thou put on habits of lamentation, and abide alone. And do thou return most austerely to the practice of Liber Jugorum, testing thyself by a standard higher than that hitherto accomplished, and punishing effractions with a heavier goad. Nor do thou return to thy devotion until that body and mind are tamed and trained to all manner of peaceable going.

36. *Concerning minor methods adjuvant in the ceremonies.* *I. Rising on the planes.* By this method mayst thou assist the imagination at the time of concluding thine Invocation. Act as taught in Liber O, by the light of Liber 777.

37. *Concerning minor methods adjuvant in the ceremonies.* *II. Talismanic magic.* Having made by thine Ingenium a talisman or pantacle to represent the particular Deity, and

53

consecrated it with infinite love and care, do thou burn it ceremonially before the shrine, as if thereby giving up the shadow for the substance. But it is useless to do this unless thou do really in thine heart value the talisman beyond all else that thou hast.

38. *Concerning minor methods adjuvant in the ceremonies. III. Rehearsal.* It may assist if the traditional history of the particular Deity be rehearsed before him; perhaps this is best done in dramatic form. This method is the main one recommended in the " Exercitios Espirituales " of St Ignatius, whose work may be taken as a model. Let the Philosophus work out the legend of his own particular Deity, and apportioning days to events, live that life in imagination, exercising the five senses in turn, as occasion arises.

39. *Concerning minor matters adjuvant in the ceremonies. IV. Duresse.* This method consists in cursing a deity recalcitrant; as, threatening ceremonially "to burn the blood of Osiris, and to grind down his bones to powder." This method is altogether contrary to the spirit of love, unless the particular Deity be himself savage and relentless; as, Jehovah or Kali. In such a case the desire to perform constraint and cursing may be the sign of the assimilation of the spirit of the devotee with that of his God, and so an advance to the Union with Him.

40. *Concerning the value of this particular form of Union or Samadhi.* All Samadhi is defined as the ecstatic union of subject and object in consciousness, with the result that a third thing arises which partakes in no way of the nature of the two.

It would seem at first sight that it is of no importance

54

LIBER ASTARTÉ

whatever to choose an object of meditation. For example, the Samadhi called Atmadarshana might arise from simple concentration of the thought on an imagined triangle, or on the heart.

But as the union of two bodies in chemistry may be endothermic or exothermic, the combination of Oxygen with Nitrogen is gentle, while that of Oxygen with Hydrogen is explosive; and as it is found that the most heat is disengaged as a rule by the union of bodies most opposite in character, and that the compound resulting from such is most stable, so it seems reasonable to suggest that the most important and enduring Samadhi results from the contemplation of the Object most opposite to the devotee. [On other planes, it has been suggested that the most opposed types make the best marriages and produce the healthiest children. The greatest pictures and operas are those in which violent extremes are blended, and so generally in every field of activity. Even in mathematics, the greatest parallelogram is formed if the lines composing it are set at right angles. ED.]

41. *Conclusions from the foregoing.* It may then be suggested to the Philosophus, that although his work will be harder his reward will be greater if he choose a Deity most remote from his own nature. This method is harder and higher than that of Liber E. For a simple object as there suggested is of the same nature as the commonest things of life, while even the meanest Deity is beyond uninitiated human understanding. On the same plane, too, Venus is nearer to man than Aphrodite, Aphrodite than Isis, Isis than Babalon, Babalon than Nuit.

Let him decide therefore according to his discretion on the

55

one hand and his aspiration on the other: and let not one outrun his fellow.

42. *Further concerning the value of this Method.* Certain objections arise. Firstly, in the nature of all human love is illusion, and a certain blindness. Nor is there any true love below the Veil of the Abyss. For this reason We give this Method to the Philosophus, as the reflection of the Exempt Adept, who reflects the Magister Templi and the Magus. Let then the Philosophus attain this method as a foundation of the higher Methods to be given to him when he attains those higher grades.

Another objection lies in the partiality of this Method. This is equally a defect characteristic of the Grade.

43. *Concerning a notable danger of Success.* It may occur that owing to the tremendous power of the Samadhi, overcoming all other memories as it should and does do, that the mind of the devotee may be obsessed, so that he declare his particular Deity to be sole God and Lord. This error has been the foundation of all dogmatic religions, and so the cause of more misery than all other errors combined.

The Philosophus is peculiarly liable to this because from the nature of the Method he cannot remain sceptical; he must for the time believe in his particular Deity. But let him (1) consider that this belief is only a weapon in his hands, (2) affirm sufficiently that his Deity is but an emanation or reflection or eidolon of a Being beyond him, as was said in Paragraph 2. For if he fail herein, since man cannot remain permanently in Samadhi, the memorised Image in his mind will be degraded, and replaced by the corresponding Demon, to his utter ruin.

56

Therefore, after Success, let him not delight overmuch in his Deity, but rather busy himself with his other work, not permitting that which is but a step to become a goal. As it is written also, Liber CLXXXV.: " remembering that Philosophy is the Equilibrium of him that is in the House of Love."

44. *Concerning secrecy, and the rites of Blood.* During this practice it is most wise that the Philosophus utter no word concerning his working, as if it were a Forbidden Love that consumeth him. But let him answer fools according to their folly; for since he cannot conceal his love from his fellows, he must speak to them as they may understand.

And as many Deities demand sacrifices, one of men, another of cattle, a third of doves, let these sacrifices be replaced by the true sacrifices in thine own heart. Yet if thou must symbolise them outwardly for the hardness of thine heart, let thine own blood, and not another's, be spilt before that altar.[1]

Nevertheless, forget not that this practice is dangerous, and may cause the manifestation of evil things, hostile and malicious, to thy great hurt.

45. *Concerning a further sacrifice.* Of this it shall be understood that nothing is to be spoken ; nor need anything be spoken to him that hath wisdom to comprehend the number of the paragraph. And this sacrifice is fatal beyond all, unless it be a sacrifice indeed. Yet there are those who have dared and achieved thereby.

46. *Concerning yet a further sacrifice.* Here it is spoken of actual mutilation. Such acts are abominable ; and while

[1] The exceptions to this rule pertain neither to this practice, nor to this grade. N. Fra. A∴A∴

57

they may bring success in this Method, form an absolute bar to all further progress.

And they are in any case more likely to lead to madness than to Samadhi. He indeed who purposeth them is already mad.

47. *Concerning human affection.* During this practice thou shalt in no wise withdraw thyself from human relations, only figuring to thyself that thy father or thy brother or thy wife is as it were an image of thy particular Deity. Thus shall they gain, and not lose, by thy working. Only in the case of thy wife this is difficult, since she is more to thee than all others, and in this case thou mayst act with temperance, lest her personality overcome and destroy that of thy Deity.

48. *Concerning the Holy Guardian Angel.* Do thou in no wise confuse this invocation with that.

49. *The Benediction.* And so may the Love that passeth all Understanding keep your hearts and minds through IΑΩ ΑΔΩΝΑΙ CΑΒΑΩ and through BABALON of the City of the Pyramids, and through Astarté the Starry One green-girdled in the name ARARITA. AMN.

58

LIBER NV

SVB FIGVRÅ

XI

A∴A∴
Publication in Class D
(for Winners of the Ordeal X.).
Imprimatur:
ᗡᗡᗡ · · ·
V.V.V.V.V. . . .
N. Fra A∴A∴
O.M. $7° = 4°$.

LIBER NV

SVB FIGVRÂ XI

000. This is the Book of the Cult of the Infinite Without.

00. The Aspirant is Hadit. Nuit is the infinite expansion of the Rose; Hadit the infinite concentration of the Rood. (*Instruction of V.V.V.V.V.*)

0. First let the Aspirant learn in his heart the First Chapter of the Book of the Law. (*Instruction of V.V.V.V.V.*)

1. Worship, *i.e.* identify thyself with, the Khabs, the secret Light within the Heart. Within this, again, unextended, is Hadit.

This is the first practice of Meditation (ccxx. I. 6 and 21).

2. Adore and understand the Rim of the Stélé of Revealing.

> " Above, the gemmed azure is
> The naked splendour of Nuit;
> She bends in ecstasy to kiss
> The secret ardours of Hadit."

This is the first practice of Intelligence (ccxx. I. 14).

3. Avoid any act of choice or discrimination.

This is the first practice of Ethics (ccxx. I. 22).

13

4. Consider of six and fifty that $50 \div 6 = 0.12$.

    o the circumference, Nuit.

    . the centre, Hadit.

    1 the unity proceeding, Ra-Hoor-Khuit.

    2 the world of illusion.

    Nuit thus comprehends All in None.

    Also $50 + 6 = 56 = 5 + 6 = 11$, the key of all Rituals.

    And $50 \times 6 = 300$, the Spirit of the Child within.

(Note $NF_{us} = 72$, the Shemhamphorash and the Quinaries of the Zodiac, etc.)

This is the second practice of Intelligence (ccxx. I. 24, 25).

5. The Result of this Practice is the Consciousness of the Continuity of Existence, the Omnipresence of the Body of Nuit.

In other words, the Aspirant is conscious only of the Infinite Universe as a single Being. (Note for this the importance of Paragraph 3. ED.)

This is the first Indication of the Nature of the Result (ccxx. I. 26).

6. Meditate upon Nuit as the Continuous One resolved into None and Two as the phases of her being.

[For the Universe being self-contained must be capable of expression by the formula $(n - n) = 0$. For if not, let it be expressed by the formula $n - m = p$. That is, the Infinite moves otherwise than within itself, which is absurd. ED.]

This is the second practice of Meditation (ccxx. I. 27).

7. Meditate upon the facts of Samadhi on all planes, the liberation of heat in chemistry, joy in natural history, Ananda

14

in religion, when two things join to lose themselves in a third.

This is the third practice of Meditation (ccxx. I. 28, 29, 30).

8. Let the Aspirant pay utmost reverence to the Authority of the A∴A∴ and follow Its instructions, and let him swear a great Oath of Devotion unto Nuit.

This is the second practice of Ethics (ccxx. I. 32).

9. Let the Aspirant beware of the slightest exercise of his will against another being. Thus, lying is a better posture than sitting or standing, as it opposes less resistance to gravitation. Yet his first duty is to the force nearest and most potent ; *e.g.* he may rise to greet a friend.

This is the third practice of Ethics (ccxx. I. 41).

10. Let the Aspirant exercise his will without the least consideration for any other being. This direction cannot be understood, much less accomplished, until the previous practice has been perfected.

This is the fourth practice of Ethics (ccxx. I. 42, 43, 44).

11. Let the Aspirant comprehend that these two practices are identical.

This is the third practice of Intelligence (ccxx. I. 45).

12. Let the Aspirant live the Life Beautiful and Pleasant. For this freedom hath he won. But let each act, especially of love, be devoted wholly to his true mistress, Nuit.

This is the fifth practice of Ethics (ccxx. I. 51, 52, 61, 63).

13. Let the Aspirant yearn toward Nuit under the stars of Night, with a love directed by his Magical Will, not merely proceeding from the heart.

This is the first practice of Magick Art (ccxx. I. 57).

15

14. The Result of this Practice in the subsequent life of the Aspirant is to fill him with unimaginable joys : to give him certainty concerning the nature of the phenomenon called death ; to give him peace unalterable, rest, and ecstasy.

This is the second Indication of the Nature of the Result (ccxx. I. 58).

15. Let the Aspirant prepare a perfume of resinous woods and gums, according to his inspiration.

This is the second practice of Magick Art (ccxx. I. 59).

16. Let the Aspirant prepare a Pantacle, as follows.

Inscribe a circle within a Pentagram, upon a ground square or of such other convenient shape as he may choose. Let the circle be scarlet, the Pentagram black, the ground royal blue studded with golden stars.

Within the circle, at its centre, shall be painted a sigil that shall be revealed to the Aspirant by Nuit Herself.

And this Pentacle shall serve for a Telismatic Image, or as an Eidolon, or as a Focus for the mind.

This is the third practice of Magick Art (ccxx. I. 60).

17. Let the Aspirant find a lonely place, if possible a place in the Desert of Sand, or if not, a place unfrequented, and without objects to disturb the view. Such are moorlands, fens, the open sea, broad rivers, and open fields. Also, and especially, the summits of mountains.

There let him invoke the Goddess as he hath Wisdom and Understanding so to do. But let this Invocation be that of a pure heart, *i.e.* a heart wholly devoted to Her, and let him remember that it is Hadit Himself in the most secret place thereof that invoketh. Then let this serpent Hadit burst into flame.

16

LIBER NV

This is the fourth practice of Magick Art (ccxx. I. 61.

18. Then shall the Aspirant come a little to lie in Her bosom.

This is the third Indication of the Nature of the Result (ccxx. I. 61).

19. Let the Aspirant stand upon the edge of a precipice in act or in imagination. And let him imagine and suffer the fear of falling.

Next let him imagine with this aid that the Earth is falling, and he with it, or he from it; and considering the infinity of space, let him excite the fear within him to the point of ecstasy, so that the most dreadful dream of falling that he hath ever suffered be as nothing in comparison.

This is the fourth practice of Meditation. (Instruction of V.V.V.V.V.)

20. Thus having understood the nature of this Third Indication, let him in his Magick Rite fall from himself into Nuit, or expand into Her, as his imagination may compel him.

And at that moment, desiring earnestly the Kiss of Nuit, let him give one particle of dust, *i.e.* let Hadit give himself up utterly to Her.

This is the fifth practice of Magick Art (ccxx. I. 61).

21. Then shall he lose all in that hour.

This is the fourth Indication of the Nature of the Result (ccxx. I. 61).

22. Let the Aspirant prepare a lovesong of rapture unto the Goddess, or let him be inspired by Her unto this.

This is the sixth practice of Magick Art (ccxx. 63).

23. Let the Aspirant be clad in a single robe. An

17

"abbai" of scarlet wrought with gold is most suitable. (The abbai is not unlike the Japanese kimono. It must fold simply over the breast without belt or other fastening. ED.)

This is the seventh practice of Magick Art (ccxx. I. 61).

24. Let the Aspirant wear a rich head-dress. A crown of gold adorned with sapphires or diamonds with a royal blue cap of maintenance, or nemmes, is most suitable.

This is the eighth practice of Magick Art (ccxx. I. 61).

25. Let the Aspirant wear many jewels such as he may possess.

This is the ninth practice of Magick Art (ccxx. I. 63).

26. Let the Aspirant prepare an Elixir or libation as he may have wit to do.

This is the tenth practice of Magick Art (ccxx. I. 63).

27. Let the Aspirant invoke, lying supine, his robe spread out as it were a carpet.

This is the eleventh practice of Magick Art. (Instruction of V.V.V.V.V.)

28. Summary.   Preliminaries.

These are the necessary possessions.

1. The Crown or head-dress.
2. The Jewels.
3. The Pantacle.
4. The Robe.
5. The Song or Incantation.
6. The Place of Invocation.
7. The Perfume.
8. The Elixir.

18

LIBER NV

29. Summary continued.   Preliminaries.
These are the necessary comprehensions.
1. The Natures of Nuit and Hadit, and their relation.
2. The Mystery of the Individual Will.
30. Summary continued.   Preliminaries.
These are the meditations necessary to be accomplished.
1. The discovery of Hadit in the Aspirant, and indentification with Him.
2. The Continuous One.
3. The value of the Equation $n + (-n)$.
4. Cremnophobia.
31. Summary continued.   Preliminaries.
These are the Ethical Practices to be accomplished.
1. Assertion of Kether-point-of-view.
2. Reverence to the Order.
3. Abolition of human will.
4. Exercise of true will.
5. Devotion to Nuit throughout a beautified life.
32. Summary continued.   The Actual Rite.
1. Retire to desert with crown and other insignia and implements.
2. Burn perfume.
3. Chant incantation.
4. Drink unto Nuit of the Elixir.
5. Lying supine, with eyes fixed on the stars, practice the sensation of falling into nothingness.
6. Being actually within the bosom of Nuit, let Hadit surrender Himself.

19

33. Summary concluded. The Results.

    1. Expansion of consciousness to that of the Infinite.

    2. " Loss of all" the highest mystical attainment.

    3. True Wisdom and Perfect Happiness.

20

LIBER H A D

SVB FIGVRÂ

DLV

A.·.A.·.

Publication in Class D

(for Winners of the Ordeal X).

Imprimatur:

ᓂᓂᓂ · · ·

V.V.V.V.V. . . . .

N. Fra A.·.A.·.

O.M. $7° = 4°$.

LIBER H A D

SVB FIGVÂRA DLV

ooo. This is the Book of the Cult of the Infinite Within.

oo. The Aspirant is Nuit. Nuit is the infinite expansion of the Rose; Hadit the infinite concentration of the Rood. (*Instruction of V.V.V.V.V.*)

o. First let the Aspirant learn in his heart the Second Chapter of the Book of the Law. (*Instruction of V.V.V.V.V.*)

1. Worship, *i.e.* identify thyself with, Nuit, as a lambent flame of blue, all-touching, all-penetrant, her lovely hands upon the black earth, and her lithe body arched for love, and her soft feet not hurting the little flowers, even as She is imaged in the Stélé of Revealing.

This is the first practice of Meditation (ccxx. I. 26).

2. Let him further identify himself with the heart of Nuit, whose ecstasy is in that of her children, and her joy to see their joy, who sayeth : I love you ! I yearn to you. Pale or purple, veiled or voluptuous, I who am all pleasure and purple, and drunkenness of the innermost sense, desire you. Put on the wings, and arouse the coiled splendour within you. Come unto me ! . . . Sing the rapturous love-song unto me ! Burn to me perfumes ! Wear to me jewels ! Drink to me, for I love you ! I love you ! I am the blue-lidded daughter of

85

Sunset; I am the naked brilliance of the voluptuous night-sky. To me! To me!

This is the second practice of Meditation (ccxx. I. 13, 61, 63, 64, 65).

3. Let the Aspirant apply himself to comprehend Hadit as an unextended point clothed with Light ineffable. And let him beware lest he be dazzled by that Light.

This is the first practice of Intelligence (ccxx. II. 2).

4. Let the Aspirant apply himself to comprehend Hadit as the ubiquitous centre of every sphere conceivable.

This is the second practice of Intelligence (ccxx. II. 3).

5. Let the Aspirant apply himself to comprehend Hadit as the soul of every man, and of every star, conjoining this in his Understanding with the Word (*ccxx. I.* 2). "Every man and every woman is a star." Let this conception be that of Life, the giver of Life, and let him perceive that therefore the knowledge of Hadit is the knowledge of death.

This is the third practice of Intelligence (ccxx. II. 6).

6. Let the Aspirant apply himself to comprehend Hadit as the Magician or maker of Illusion, and the Exorcist or destroyer of Illusion, under the figure of the axle of the Wheel, and the cube in the circle. Also as the Universal Soul of Motion.

(This conception harmonises Thoth and Harpocrates in a very complete and miraculous manner. Thoth is both the Magus of Taro (see Lib. 418) and the Universal Mercury; Harpocrates both the destroyer of Typhon and the Babe on the Lotus. Note that the "Ibis position" formulates this conception most exactly. ED.)

This is the fourth practice of Intelligence (ccxx. II. 7).

86

7. Let the Aspirant apply himself to comprehend Hadit as the perfect, that is Not, and solve the mystery of the numbers of Hadit and his components by his right Ingenium.

This is the fifth practice of Intelligence (ccxx. II. 15, 16).

8. Let the Aspirant, bearing him as a great King, root out and destroy without pity all things in himself and his surroundings which are weak, dirty, or diseased, or otherwise unworthy. And let him be exceeding proud and joyous.

This is the first practice of Ethics (ccxx. II. 18, 19, 20, 21).

9. Let the Aspirant apply himself to comprehend Hadit as the Snake that giveth Knowledge and Delight and bright glory, who stirreth the hearts of men with drunkenness. This snake is blue and gold; its eyes are red, and its spangles green and ultra-violet.

(That is, as the most exalted form of the Serpent Kundalini.)

This is the sixth practice of Intelligence (ccxx. II. 22, 50, 51).

10. Let him further identify himself with this Snake.

This is the second practice of Meditation (ccxx. II. 22).

11. Let the Aspirant take wine and strange drugs, according to his knowledge and experience, and be drunk thereof.

(The Aspirant should be in so sensitive a condition that a single drop, perhaps even the smell, should suffice. ED.)

This is the first practice of Magick Art (ccxx. II. 22).

12. Let the Aspirant concentrate his consciousness in the Rood Cross set up upon the Mountain, and identify himself with It. Let him be well aware of the difference between Its

87

own soul, and that thought which it habitually awakes in his own mind.

This is the third practice of Meditation, and as it will be found, a comprehension and harmony and absorption of the practices of Intelligence (ccxx. II. 22).

13. Let the Aspirant apply himself to comprehend Hadit as the Unity which is the Negative. (Ain Elohim. ED.)

This is the seventh practice of Intelligence (ccxx. II. 23).

14. Let the Aspirant live the life of a strong and beautiful being, proud and exalted, contemptuous of and fierce toward all that is base and vile.

This is the second practice of Ethics (ccxx. II. 24, 25, 45-49, 52, 56-60).

15. Let the Aspirant apply himself to comprehend Hadit according to this 26th verse of the Second Chapter of the Book of the Law. And this shall be easy for him if he have well accomplished the Third Practice of Meditation.

This is the eighth practice of Intelligence (ccxx. II. 26).

16. Let the Aspirant destroy Reason in himself according to the practice in Liber CDLXXIV.

This is the fourth practice of Meditation (ccxx. II. 27-33).

17. Let the Aspirant observe duly the Feasts appointed by the A∴A∴ and perform such rituals of the elements as he possesseth, invoking them duly in their season.

This is the second practice of Magick Art (ccxx. II. 35-43).

18. Let the Aspirant apply himself to comprehend Hadit as a babe in the egg of the Spirit (Akasha. ED.) that is invisible within the 4 elements.

This is the ninth practice of Intelligence (ccxx. II. 49).

88

LIBER H A D

19. The Aspirant seated in his Asana will suddenly commence to breathe strangely, and this without the Operation of his will; the Inspiration will be associated with the thought of intense excitement and pleasure, even to exhaustion; and the Expiration very rapid and forceful, as if this excitement were suddenly released.

This is the first and last Indication of the Sign of the Beginning of this Result (ccxx. II. 63).

20. A light will appear to the Aspirant, unexpectedly. Hadit will arise within him, and Nuit concentrate Herself upon him from without. He will be overcome, and the Conjunction of the Infinite Without with the Infinite Within will take place in his soul, and the One be resolved into the None.

This is the first Indication of the Nature of the Result (ccxx. II. 61, 62, 64).

21. Let the Aspirant strengthen his body by all means in his power, and let him with equal pace refine all that is in him to the true ideal of Royalty. Yet let his formula, as a King's ought, be Excess.

This is the third practice of Ethics (ccxx. II. 70, 71).

22. To the Aspirant who succeeds in this practice the result goes on increasing until its climax in his physical death in its due season. This practice should, however, prolong life.

This is the second Indication of the Nature of the Result (ccxx. II. 66, 72-74).

23. Let the Adept aspire to the practice of Liber XI. and preach to mankind.

This is the fourth Practice of Ethics (ccxx. II. 76).

89

24. Let the Adept worship the Name, foursquare, mystic, wonderful, of the Beast, and the name of His house; and give blessing and worship to the prophet of the lovely Star.

This is the fifth practice of Ethics (ccxx. II. 78, 79).

25. Let the Aspirant expand his consciousness to that of Nuit, and bring it rushing inward. It may be practised by imagining that the Heavens are falling, and then transferring the consciousness to them.

This is the fifth practice of Meditation. (Instruction of V.V.V.V.V.)

26. Summary. Preliminaries.
These are the necessary possessions.
   1. Wine and strange drugs.

27. Summary continued. Preliminaries.
These are the necessary comprehensions.
   1. The nature of Hadit (and of Nuit, and the relations between them.)

28. Summary continued. Preliminaries.
These are the meditations necessary to be accomplished.
   1. Identification with Nuit, body and spirit.
   2. Identification with Hadit as the Snake.
   3. Identification with Hadit as the Rood Cross.
   4. Destruction of Reason.
   5. The Falling of the Heavens.

29. Summary continued. Preliminaries.
These are the Ethical Practices to be accomplished.
   1. The destruction of all unworthiness in one's self and one's surroundings.
   2. Fulness, almost violence, of life.

90

30. Summary continued. Preliminaries.

These are the Magick Arts to be practised.

    1. During the preparation, perform the Invocations of the Elements.

    2. Observe the Feasts appointed by the A∴ A∴.

31. Summary continued. The actual Practice.

    1. Procure the suitable intoxication.

    2. As Nuit, contract thyself with infinite force upon Hadit.

32. Summary continued. The Results.

    1. Peculiar automatic breathing begins.

    2. A light appears.

    3. Samadhi of the two Infinites within aspirant.

    4. Intensification of 3 on repetition.

    5. Prolongation of life.

    6. Death becomes the climax of the practice.

33. Summary concluded.

These are the practices to be performed in token of Thanksgiving for success.

    1. Aspiration to Liber XI.

    2. Preaching of Θελημα to mankind.

    3. Blessing and Worship to the prophet of the lovely Star.

91

TWO FRAGMENTS OF RITUAL

[Translated by Fra. K. Φ. IX°. from a German MS. said to have been found among the papers of Weishaupt. It by no means appears that the fragments pertain to the Illuminati ; Weishaupt's MS. was probably a mere transcript from some older ritual which he valued on purely archæological grounds.—ED.]

81

TWO FRAGMENTS OF RITUAL

I

THE SUPREME RITUAL

" A feast for the Supreme Ritual."
" To him is the winged secret flame, and to her the stooping starlight."
                                                                —*Liber Legis.*

LET a feast be made by the Officers of the Temple. This Temple, into which they then retire, may be any convenient place. An altar is necessary ; also a vessel of wine ; otherwise as may be appointed by them : *e.g.* the robes, etc., as said in . . . . The Officers are two in number, and seek Nuit and Hadit through Babalon and the Beast.[1] To conceal themselves, they are disguised as Isis and Osiris.

[*The officers meet and clasp hands above the altar. Any preliminary operations, such as opening, banishing, etc., are now done by* I.,[2] *who returns, and they again greet, but as initiates.*]

    o. and I. [*face to face*].

    o. What is the hour?

    I. When time hath no power.

    o. What is the place?

    I. At the limits of space.

    o. What God do we wake?

[1] This is the nearest idea I can give of the text, which is in hieroglyph impossible to reproduce.

[2] It is clear that this ritual is full of intentional blinds.

83

i. The L . . . of the S . . . .!

o. With what do we serve?

i. B . . . . ., M . . . . ., and N . . . .!

o. The shrine in the gloom?

[*Gives the S . . . of a B . . . of the A . . . ., which* i.
destroys by the S . . . of M . . T . the God.

i. Is the M . . . . O . T . . W . . .

o. And the Priest in the Shrine?

i. Is this M . . . . . . O . M . . .!

[i. *repeats S . . . of M . . T . and O. gives S . . . of Baphomet.*

o. And the wonder above?

i. The Quintessence of Love.

o. There are sacraments?

i.   Nine.

There are music and wine
And the delicate dance—

o. To accomplish?

i.   The trance.

o. And are these three enough?

i. They are servants of Love.

o. And the sacrifice?

i.   I.

o. And the priestess?

i.   Is thou.

I am willing to die
At thy hands—even now.

o. Worship me first!

[i. *seats* o. *upon the Altar.*

i. Mistress, I thirst.

[o. *gives wine. They drink.*

84

o. My mouth is on fire
To my lord's desire.
   [*They exchange the holy greeting by a kiss.*
i. I kneel at thy feet,
And the honey is sweet.
   [o. *plays music while* i *worships in silence.*
o. Exhausted, I sink.
i. I am dead, on the brink.
o. Let us dance!
i.   Let us dance!
o. i. The Lord give us power
To be lost in the trance
For an hour—for an hour!
[*They dance together. A pause of perfect stillness and
silence follows; until O.,* sua sponte, *advances and places*
i. *upon the altar.*
o. Exhaust me!
i.   Nay, drink!
o. Ere I sink!
i.   I shall sink!
o. Drink wine! oh, drink wine!
i. I am thine!
o.   I am thine!
   [*They drink and greet as before.*
i. Art thou armed?
o.   With a knife.
   [o. *draws the dagger from her hair.*
i. Love is better than life.
[o. *cuts a* ⊥, *or if possible, the Sigil of N. O. X., on* i.'s *breast.*
o. Let us dance!

85

1. [*giving wine.*] To the trance!

    [*They drink, then dance.*

o. Back to the throne!

    [I. *returns, and takes seat thereon.*

1. I adore thee alone!

[o. *does so, plays music if so inclined, and continues as necessity or inclination may dictate.*

o. It is ended, the play:
    I am ready to slay.
    Anoint me!

1.   I rise
    To the fire of thine eyes.
    I anoint thee, thy priest,
    Babalon—and The Beast!
    And I ask of Thee now:
    Who art Thou?

o. Omari tessala marax etc.

[*The Ritual of the S. . . . of R. . . . is in silence accomplished.*

IX°

CLOSING

1. Mouth to mouth and heart to heart!
o. For the moment we must part.
1. Time and space renew the illusion.
o. Love is swallowed in confusion.
1. Love sustains us eminent
    Till the hour of Sacrament.
o. I love you, and you love me.
1. Now and ever may it be!
1. and o. Hand in hand is heart to heart.
    Love be with us, though we part.

    [*They greet, as before, and depart.*

86

II

A RITUAL TO INVOKE

HICE

OR ANY OTHER DIVINE ONE

THE OPENING

The assistants being all without, N. *and* H. *perform the ritual appropriate. The doors are unlocked, and the assistants, led by* R., *enter.*

LET the symbol or image of $\left\{ \begin{array}{l} \text{the god} \\ \text{HICE} \end{array} \right\}$ be in the East of the Temple.

Let incense burn before $\left\{ \begin{array}{l} \text{it.} \\ \text{her.} \end{array} \right.$

Let there be two other thrones : on her right that of Nuit, on her left that of Hadit ; the child is Ra Hoor Khuit.

Nuit is dressed in blue, Hadit in red ; the child is . . .

[*MS. torn here.*

The lamp shall be burning above R.H.K., who crouches in the centre, in the prescribed posture.

If they be assistants, they shall all wear the robes of their grade ; they shall be seated in balanced disposition about the temple ; and they shall enter only after the opening.

THE OPENING

H. Knock as appropriate to god invoked.

N. The Hymn appropriate to banishing.

87

H. The Banishing Ritual of the ⛤, as revised.

N. B. . . . . . . !

H. O. . . . . . !

THE DEATH OF OSIRIS

H. *and* N. *divest themselves of their blue and red robes, appearing merely in their magick robes of red and green as the temporal and spiritual powers, Typhon and Apophis.*

H. Sister, I burn upon the throne.

N. I am in agony, Typhon !

H. Who hath disturbed our ageless peace ?

N. Threatened our mystery ?

H.   Isis
Hath borne a child.

N.   We are twins.

H.   What word
Insults us ?

R. [*Springs up.*] Lo ! I am, the third.

H. [*Comes forward with the scourge, and forces* R. *to kneel.*]
Then bow thee to the two above !   [*Strikes him twice.*

N. [*Comes forward with the rod.*] We need no witness of
our love.   [*Strikes him twice.*

H. Who art thou ?

N.   Whence art thou ?

R.   My name
Is surely I am that I am.

H. Blaspheme not !   [*Strikes him twice.*

N.   Lie not !   [*Strikes him twice.*

88

R.   I am come
From Isis, from the Virgin Womb.
H. Blaspheme not!   [*Strikes him twice.*
N.   Lie not!   [*Strikes him twice.*
R.   I am he
Appointed from eternity
To rule upon the folk of Khem.
H. We are the gods and kings of them.
N. Upstart!   [*Strikes him twice.*
H.   Usurper!   [*Strikes him twice.*
N.   We defy thee.
H. We have the power to crucify thee.
        [N. *forces* R. *back, and they stretch out his arms.*
R. Amen! I am willing to be slain.
Verily I shall rise again!
N. With four wounds thus I nail thee.
        [*Wounds brow, hands, and feet with the dagger.*
H. With one wound I impale thee.
                    [*Wounds breast with sword.*
H. Hail, sister! We have slain the god.
N. Ours is the termless period.
H. Bending across the bloodless face
Let us embrace!
N.   Let us embrace!
[*They embrace, leaning across the corpse.* N. *returns to
her throne, and dons the blue robe, thus assuming the
power of Isis.* H. *remains, his sword upon the heart
of* R.

89

THE ARISING OF HORUS

N. *chants the Dirge of Isis.*[1] *After* "tomb" *in verse* 4 *she rises, and* H. *falls back to his knees. At verse* 5 N. *comes down to the corpse, and raises it with kisses upon the stigmata, wrapping it then in her blue robe.* She *then clothes it in the white robe* (of a Probationer? Trans.). R. *takes the sword of* H. *and* . . . (?) *his throat therewith.* N. *returns to her throne and* H. *rises and puts on his red robe.*

THE AWAKENING OF THE DIVINE FORCE

[*The remaining sheets of MSS. are missing or indecipherable.*

[1] MS. not to be found.

90

SEXUAL OUTLAW:
IDA CRADDOCK

Persecuted by Anthony Comstock and his Society
for the Suppression of Vice, Ida Craddock was a
turn-of-the century sex educator and spiritualist. Born
in Philadelphia in 1857, she became an occult scholar
around the age of thirty, taking classes at the Theosophi-
cal Society and studying various occult subjects. She
also taught correspondence courses to women and new-
lyweds on the importance of viewing sex as a sacred act,
and much of her knowledge of the marriage bed came to
her from her nightly visit with her angelic husband Soph.
She wrote the essay *Heavenly Bridegrooms* on this topic.

In 1902 Craddock was arrested under New York's
anti-obscenity laws. She committed suicide rather than
face life in an asylum. As Vere Chappell writes in his book
Sexual Outlaw, Erotic Mystic: The Essential Ida Craddock:

> Although it attracted little attention in the main-
> stream press, *Heavenly Bridegrooms* did catch
> the eye of the famed British occultist Aleis-
> ter Crowley. Crowley had been introduced via

correspondence to Theodore Schroeder through the American poet Harry Kemp.[1] When Crowley came to America in 1914, one of the first things he did was to write Schroeder and arrange a meeting. Crowley wanted Schroeder to organize public lectures for him in America, and Schroeder was interested in Crowley's writings on sex and religion. Crowley eventually sold him a copy of his *Bagh-i-muattar: The Scented Garden of Abdullah the Satirist of Shiraz* (1910), and even offered Schroeder access to proprietary O.T.O. documents on sexual mysticism if he would agree to join the Order and swear not to reveal its secrets. Schroeder never took him up on the offer.

It was through Schroeder that Crowley became acquainted with the ideas of Ida Craddock, with whom he was unabashedly impressed. He wrote a glowing review of *Heavenly Bridegrooms* for his occult periodical *The Equinox*. It is significant that he signed the review as "Baphomet," using his name as head of the O.T.O. in the English-speaking world, thus implicitly affirming the relevance of Craddock's work to the O.T.O.'s mysteries. (Crowley regularly wrote reviews in *The Equinox* under

---

1 Harry Kemp (1883–1960), well known as "America's tramp poet," met Crowley in London and subsequently wrote a sensationalist account of his activities for the *New York World* in 1914.

several different names, depending on the subject matter.) One of his most famous quotes also came from this review: "When you have proved that God is merely a name for the sex instinct, it appears to me not far to the perception that the sex instinct is God."

Crowley also took issue with the skepticism expressed by Schroeder in his introduction to the book, seeing no reason not to take Ida's claims at face value rather than assuming they were hallucinations. After all, Crowley was a practicing occultist who knew very well the power of the subconscious mind to communicate through visions and other mystical states. In one of his books of magical instruction, he wrote: "In this book it is spoken of the Sephiroth and the Paths; of Spirits and Conjurations; of Gods, Spheres, Planes, and many other things which may or may not exist. It is immaterial whether these exist or not. By doing certain things certain results will follow; students are most earnestly warned against attributing objective reality or philosophic validity to any of them."[2] In other words, whether or not the existence of a spirit guide or Borderland husband can be proven objectively, the important measure is the value of the

---

2 Aleister Crowley, "Liber O vel Manus et Sagittae," *The Equinox*, vol. 1, no. 2 (1909), p. 13.

experience to the mystic. In Ida Craddock's case, it is hoped that this book has provided sufficient basis for the reader to judge.

HEAVENLY BRIDEGROOMS. By THEODORE SCHROEDER and IDA C——. Reprinted from the *Alienist and Neurologist*.

THIS book has been left entirely unedited by Mr. Theodore Schroeder, with the exception of a very brief explanatory note. I may say that it is one of the most remarkable human documents ever produced, and it should certainly find a regular publisher in book form. The authoress of the MS. claims that she was the wife of an angel. She expounds at the greatest length the philosophy connected with this thesis. Her learning is enormous. She finds traces of similar beliefs in every country in the world, and (having a similar experience of her own) she can hardly be blamed for arguing that one thing confirms the other. Mr. Schroeder is quite logical in calling her paper An Unintentional Contribution to the Erotogenetic Interpretation of Religion, but commits the errors of *petitio principii* and *non distributio medii* with the most exquisite nonchalance. Only a lawyer could be so shameless. He begs the question with regard to this particular case, assuming that her relation with the angel was pure hallucination, of which he has no evidence whatever. He argues that, since one person both loves and is religious, religion is nothing but a morbid manifestation of the sexual instinct. One does not have even to disagree with him to see how worthless is his reasoning. As a matter of fact, I do half agree with him in my calmer moments in a general way, but the conclusion can be carried a step further. When you have proved that God is merely a name for the sex instinct, it appears to me not far to the perception that the sex instinct is God.

This particular MS. is absolutely sane in every line. The fact that the woman committed suicide twelve or fifteen years afterwards is no more against the sanity of the MS. than the suicide of Socrates proves that the *Republic* is merely the lucubration of a lunatic. I am very far from agreeing with all that this most talented woman sets forth in her paper, but she certainly obtained initiated knowledge of extraordinary depth. She seems to have had access to certain most concealed sanctuaries. I should personally be inclined to attribute her suicide rather to the vengeance of the guardians of those palaces than to any more obvious cause. She has put down statements in plain English which are positively staggering. This book is of incalculable value to every student of occult matters. No Magick library is complete without it.

BAPHOMET.

ABOUT THE AUTHOR

ALEISTER CROWLEY (1875–1947) poet, mountaineer, secret agent, magus, libertine, and prophet was dubbed by the tabloids "The Wickedest Man in the World."

LON MILO DUQUETTE is the author of sixteen critically acclaimed books (translated in twelve languages) on Magick and the Occult. He is the U.S. Deputy Grandmaster General of the O.T.O. He lives in Costa Mesa, California with his wife of 45 years, Constance.

ABOUT THE SERIES

The Equinox, in print from 1909–1919, was a magical journal published by Aleister Crowley and included instructions for Crowley's own magical Order, the A∴A∴ as well as important exercises, meditations, rituals, reviews, and works by other magical adepts. Originally published as ten volumes, much of the material remains out of print today. Now, for the first time since Israel Regardie's 1974 release of *Gems from the Equinox,* renowned scholar and U.S. Deputy Grandmaster General of the O.T.O. Lon Milo DuQuette presents readers with his own selections from this classic publication, *The Best of the Equinox.*

From *The Best of the Equinox,* *Enochian Magick: Volume I*

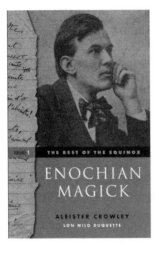

Volume I presents readers with the Enochian magic selections from *The Equinox* and contains Crowley's practical distillation of the work of Elizabethan magi John Dee and Edward Kelley—perhaps the most powerful and elegant of all magical systems. Dee and Kelley's work is one of the most popular magical techniques seized upon by modern magicians.

From the introduction:

The two major branches of modern practical Enochian Magic (Elemental and Aethyrical) were grafted by Mathers into the Adeptus Minor curriculum of the Golden Dawn. In 1898, Aleister Crowley joined the Golden Dawn and in 1900 attained the grade of Adeptus Minor. The passion of his exploration of the Enochian system far exceeded the efforts of his predecessors and in 1909, while walking across the North Africa Sahara, he completed his systematic explorations of the thirty worlds of the Aethyrs and chronucked them in his masterpiece, *The Vison and the Voice.* Hermetic scholars have seriously compared this document to the visionary works of William Blake and the prophetic writings of Ezekiel and Saint John the Divine.

It would be over three hundred years before the material Dee and Kelly labored so hard to obtain would be organized into a magical system by Golden Dawn genius, S.L. MacGregor Mathers who recognized the intrinsic value of the surviving diary material. The records found in *A True and Faithful Relation . . .* supplied the bulk of this information.

The two major branches of modern practical Enochian Magic (Elemental and Aethyrical) were grafted by Mathers into the Adeptus Minor curriculum of the Golden Dawn. In 1898, Aleister Crowley joined the Golden Dawn and in 1900 attained the Grade of Adeptus Minor. The passion of his exploration of the Enochian system far exceeded the efforts of his predecessors and in 1909, while walking across the North African Sahara, he completed his systematic explorations of the thirty worlds of the Aethyrs and chronicled them in his masterpiece, *The Vision and the Voice.* Hermetic scholars have seriously compared this document to the visionary works of William Blake and the prophetic writings of Ezekiel and Saint John the Divine.

From *The Best of the Equinox, Dramatic Ritual: Volume II*

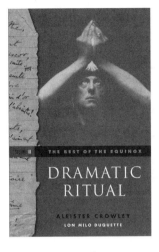

Volume II brings readers the collected works on Dramatic Rituals. More than costumes and play-acting with magical intent, dramatic rituals serve a high purpose in working magick. As Crowley wrote in *Magick in Theory and Practice,* "The object of them is almost invariably the invocation of a God, and that God conceived in a more or less material and personal fashion. These Rituals are therefore well suited for such persons as are capable of understanding the spirit of Magick as opposed to the letter."

The Best of the Equinox, Dramatic Rituals is a treasure chest of rituals suitable for performance by the solitary practitioner, as well as small and large groups of magicians and initiates. Used with skill, dramatic ritual can trigger profound consciousness-expanding and self-transformational experiences.

From the introduction:

In October and November of 1910 E.V. Crowley, with the assistance of Waddell, Neuburg, and a handful of disciples, publicly presented a series of dramatic rituals entititled THE RITES OF ELEUSIS. They were performed on seven consecutive Wednesday nights at Caxton Hall, Westminster. London had never seen anything quite like it before. The title notwithstanding, these rituals were not attempts to reenact the ancient ceremonies of the Eleusinian mysteries. In fact, the only thing Crowley's Rites of Eleusis had in common with their namesake was the simple fact that they (like their original ceremonies) were written and performed in order to evoke a specific variety of ecstasy in the participants and the audience.

From the "Rite of Luna":

THE RITES OF ELEUSIS

Whether a snake or a sun
 In his horoscope Heaven hath cast,
It is nothing ; every one
 Shall win to the moon at last.

The mage has wrought by his art
 A billion shapes in the sun.
Look through to the heart of his heart,
 And the many are shapes of one !
An end to the art of the mage,
 And the cold grey blank of the prison !
An end to the adamant age !
 The ambrosial moon is arisen.

I have bought a lily-white goat
    For the price of a crown of thorns,
A collar of gold for its throat,
    A scarlet bow for its horns ;
I have bought a lark in the lift
    For the price of a butt of sherry :
With these, and God for a gift,
    It needs no wine to be merry !

I have bought for a wafer of bread
    A garden of poppies and clover ;
For a water bitter and dead,
    A foam of fire flowing over.
From the Lamb and his prison fare
    And the Owl's blind stupor, arise !
Be ye wise, and strong, and fair,
    And the nectar afloat in your eyes !

Arise, O ambrosial moon,
    By the strong immemorial spell,
By the subtle veridical rune
    That is mighty in heaven and hell !
Drip thy mystical dews
    On the tongues of the tender fauns,
In the shade of initiate yews,
    Remote from the desert dawns !

To Our Readers

Weiser Books, an imprint of Red Wheel/Weiser, publishes books across the entire spectrum of occult, esoteric, speculative, and New Age subjects. Our mission is to publish quality books that will make a difference in people's lives without advocating any one particular path or field of study. We value the integrity, originality, and depth of knowledge of our authors.

Our readers are our most important resource, and we appreciate your input, suggestions, and ideas about what you would like to see published.

Visit our website at *www.redwheelweiser.com* to learn about our upcoming books and free downloads, and be sure to go to *www.redwheelweiser.com/newsletter/* to sign up for newsletters and exclusive offers.

You can also contact us at *info@redwheelweiser.com* or at

Red Wheel/Weiser, LLC
665 Third Street, Suite 400
San Francisco, CA 94107